SHOOT FIRST PASS LATER

MY LIFE, NO FILTER

SHOOT FIRST
PASS LATER
MY LIFE, NO FILTER

Jeremy Roenick
with **Kevin Allen**

TRIUMPH
B O O K S

This book is available in quantity at special discounts for your group or organization. For further information, contact:

Triumph Books LLC
814 N. Franklin
Chicago, Illinois 60610
(312) 337-0747
www.triumphbooks.com
@TriumphBooks

Printed in U.S.A.
ISBN: 978-1-62937-162-7
Page production by Patricia Frey
Photos courtesy of Jeremy Roenick unless otherwise indicated

CONTENTS

FOREWORD

One of the craziest events I witnessed during my National Hockey League career was Jeremy Roenick trying to fight Bob Probert as if he fully intended to kick Probie's ass.

Probert was the scariest fighter in the game, and no skill player would dare challenge the big guy. If you somehow managed to become tangled up with Probert, the only sensible objective was self-preservation. The goal was simply to hang on, to survive until help arrived.

But when I was playing with Roenick on the Chicago Blackhawks, I remember looking up and seeing Roenick throwing punches at Probert like he was Mike Tyson.

The good news for Jeremy was that Probie seemed to find the situation comical. And because Probie didn't respond with his usual fury, J.R. was spared a beating.

But that situation illustrates why Roenick's teammates always had great respect for him. He didn't back down from anyone, and he was enthusiastic about every challenge he faced.

Roenick loved everything about hockey. In all of the years I've known him, I don't remember him ever complaining about any aspect of the sport.

When I met him, I knew immediately that he had a big ego. He sometimes referred to himself in the third person. But it was funny, not annoying, because he had an innocence about him that made you like him. Everyone on the Blackhawks loved J.R.

Roenick would battle with Blackhawks coach Mike Keenan, and then with Darryl Sutter after Keenan left, but that's because Roenick was young and they were trying to push him to be the best player he could be. Keenan and Sutter loved Roenick because they knew he would always answer the bell. He always played with heart. Roenick played some very physical games, particularly in his days with the Blackhawks.

I remember Roenick leveled Kelly Kisio of the San Jose Sharks with an open-ice hit one night in 1993. At first, I thought he might have killed Kisio. He caught him cutting across the ice and laid him out with what I deemed to be a good clean hit. I don't know if it would be considered a clean hit in today's game but in the 1990s, it was a clean hit. Roenick also had a goal that night and was a force all over the ice to lead us to a 4–2 win. That's how he played when he was at his best.

Jeremy and I became instant friends when he showed up in Chicago. Roenick had an aura of fun about him. When he walked into a place, he liked people to know he was there. He traveled with a small entourage but he didn't really take himself all that seriously. He would joke about it, saying this is "just the way I am." He called himself "Styles" at one point, and when he was in Arizona he had a vanity license plate that said so.

Roenick was the kind of player the NHL needed during the 1990s. Many of our top players were about as exciting as house plants. We were short on colorful characters. Roenick came along and added some pizzazz. He always had something to say. The media loved him. Every time J.R. opened his mouth, a good story flew out.

Roenick was never afraid to be bold or cocky. Before the 1996 World Cup of Hockey, Roenick called out Team Canada and star Eric Lindros. He said the Americans were coming to get the Canadians. The interesting aspect of that story was that Roenick didn't have an NHL contract that summer and decided it was too risky to play in the World Cup.

What I remember vividly was that we faced a fired-up Canadian team, with a roster full of guys who wanted to hurt us over Roenick's comments. During that game, I looked up into the stands and Roenick was sitting in the seats signing autographs. He had a line stretching up to the concourse.

Roenick came into the dressing room after the game and we all gave him grief for stirring up a hornet's nest for us. He just laughed Eventually, we laughed as well.

Roenick's popularity in Chicago was off the charts. He couldn't go anywhere without a line forming for autographs.

Nothing has changed. It's been almost 20 years since he was traded to the Phoenix Coyotes, but when he visits Chicago, he is always greeted as if he never left.

Having grown up in Chicago, I can say that Roenick's connection with the fans there reminds me of the way Bobby Hull connected with fans. They have similar personalities. They know how to relate with people. They know how to treat fans. When fans meet Hull and Roenick, they feel as if they know them. Those guys have charisma that cannot be denied.

There was friction between the Blackhawks and Roenick over a contract right before he was traded. But that has been washed away by time and the Blackhawks' recent success. Today, Chicago fans view Roenick rightly as one of the great players in the franchise's history.

Given Roenick's statistics and reputation around the NHL, I see Roenick as a player who is destined to be enshrined in the Hockey Hall of Fame.

I had hoped he and I might enter the Hall together in 2013 but it didn't happen. As I've analyzed the list of those who have entered the Hall over the past several years, I'm more convinced than ever that Roenick deserves to be there. He was among the best of the best during his era, especially when you factor in the impact he had as one of the game's most entertaining personalities. That's an intangible contribution to the game that cannot be measured by statistics.

Sooner or later, Roenick's time will come. When it happens, I will be in Toronto celebrating with him.

—Chris Chelios
Hockey Hall of Fame, 2013

INTRODUCTION

Fans frequently ask me to name a current National Hockey League player who plays the game the way I played, and I'm forever stumped by the question.

I've never seen a player who reminds me of me.

Maybe I was unique. That was true in the 1990s, during my prime seasons, when I could be entertaining on and off the ice. Who else could dash around the rink and dance with the media the way I could?

Whenever my mouth would get me in trouble, somebody would say that they threw away the mold after J.R. was created.

At the very least, I was a one-of-a-kind showman.

The current player who most resembles me in style and personality is Washington Capitals star Alex Ovechkin.

That statement probably shocks the many fans who believe I have a Cold War attitude about Russian players. Despite what you may have read or heard, I don't hate Russian players. In fact, I greatly admire the top players in Russian hockey history, including Ovechkin.

Ovechkin is a bigger man and a more skillful goal scorer than I was. I played a smarter all-around game and was a better playmaker. But our passion for the game is the same, and Ovechkin's rambunctious playing style is similar to the way I whirled around the ice like the Tasmanian Devil.

I'm proud that I always thundered up the ice as if I were leading a full cavalry charge, and my sense is that Ovechkin also loves skating with the throttle wide open. Ovechkin seems to enjoy running over people the same way I did.

And clearly, Ovechkin samples the nightlife as much as I did during my heyday.

Ovechkin and I are also similar in our willingness to speak our minds whenever we are in the mood to do so.

The media blasted Ovechkin during the second round of the 2015 NHL playoffs when he guaranteed a victory in Game 7 of a playoff series against the New York Rangers. Ovechkin's haters said that given his poor playoff history, he had no right to channel his inner Mark Messier and guarantee a victory.

Of course, I loved what Ovechkin said, because it reminded me of something I might have said if a reporter asked me what was going to happen in a Game 7.

Remember, I'm the guy who predicted Team USA was going to win the gold medal in the 1996 World Cup. I didn't end up playing because I didn't have a contract, but I'm the guy who first said we were going to win the damn gold medal. Team USA general manager Lou Lamoriello wasn't happy that I supplied Canada with bulletin board material, but as far as I was concerned, the prediction needed to be made publicly. We needed to be on record saying we intended to beat Canada.

Here is what Ovechkin said before his Game 7 against New York: "We're going to come back and win the series. We're going to play our game, and we're going to come back and we're going to play Montreal or Tampa [in the conference final]."

Those words, by themselves, would have created only a small bonfire, but earlier in the series he trash-talked Rangers goalie Henrik Lundqvist after scoring a goal against him.

"All series, baby," Ovechkin said.

Later in the series, he said the Rangers were afraid of the Capitals' offensive might. When you piled the guarantee on top of Ovi's previous comments, his body of work suddenly became the target of media criticism. The prevailing sentiment was that Ovechkin should keep his mouth shut.

Maybe it's media members who are anti-Russian. Reporters and analysts used to celebrate when I opened my mouth and let the cockiness flow. Why don't they have the same level of enjoyment when Ovechkin has something to say? It makes you wonder.

I respect Ovechkin's rants and I wish he would do it more often. It would be good for the NHL, and it would be good for his teammates to be reminded regularly how passionate he is about our sport.

What I enjoyed most of all was Ovechkin's reaction when he was told that fans and some members of the media disapproved of his guarantee.

He said he didn't care what other people think of him.

As the team's captain, Ovechkin should go strong to the microphone. His coach, Barry Trotz, said he appreciated that Ovechkin was breathing fire before a big game. And I guarantee you that his teammates were fired up to hear that Ovechkin believed they were going to kick ass and take names.

Nobody wants to hear their leader be wishy-washy, or hopeful, or merely confident. Players want to hear their leader say, "We are going to win the fucking game."

Captains are supposed to stand up and challenge themselves to carry the load. Don't ever say you hope to win. Say you *will* win. If you believe it, it'll come true.

I was proud of Ovechkin for picking up the Capitals' flag and leading the charge. It takes guts to do something like that, because he knew he would be carved up in the press if he didn't play well. He showed large balls by making that prediction.

As it turned out, Ovechkin played well but the Capitals lost. But that didn't make his guarantee any less important. His teammates will remember how badly Ovechkin wanted to win that game.

Some of my readers are going to remember that I was brutally critical of Ovechkin for his minus-35 performance during the 2013–14 season. You probably believe I'm a hypocrite. But my response to you would be that Ovechkin deserved the criticism for that minus-35 two seasons ago.

How bad do you have to be defensively when you score 51 goals and still end up at minus-35?

The answer is that a player has to be horseshit defensively.

I'm paid by NBC to be an NHL analyst. Ovechkin had a ridiculously poor season and unfortunately I had to take him to the woodshed because of that. I called him out, and I think Ovi understood.

But I saw a different Ovechkin in 2015. I saw a player who is fully committed to implementing Trotz's system. I witnessed Ovi transform himself from a goal scorer to a superstar who is trying to be both a scorer and leader.

All of the talk about how I was anti-Russian started before my criticism of Ovechkin. It had more to do with what I've had to say about Alexander Semin and Ilya Kovalchuk in the past.

Perhaps it was also fueled by my admission in my first book that I didn't have much use for my former Phoenix Coyotes teammate Oleg Tverdovsky.

As I explained, he was my all-time least favorite teammate because he wasted his tremendous talent. He had a poor attitude, and he screwed up drills time after time in practice because he refused to focus.

Weary of his attitude, one day I dropped my gloves in practice and beat the fuck out of him. The kid had probably never had a fight in his life, and he had no answer for my fury.

My issues with Semin and Kovalchuk has nothing to do with where they're from and everything to do with what I perceive to be their selfish playing style.

When the Carolina Hurricanes signed Semin to a five-year, $35 million contract in 2013, I said on the air that it was the worst signing or move in franchise history. I didn't believe Semin would work hard enough to earn that money. I viewed him as a selfish player, a player who puts his interests above the team's best interests.

That was based on watching him play, not on his passport. I've seen him abandon a back check to leave the ice, even though it created an odd-man rush against his team.

I've witnessed Kovalchuk do that as well, and I've also seen Kovalchuk not back check because he was busy scolding his teammate for not passing him the puck on a 2-on-1 break. It was during a game against the Los Angeles Kings, and the Kings scored on the play.

Those are selfish plays, and I'm sure a Russian coach would have been just as disgusted at those players as their NHL counterparts were.

The truth is that I've marveled at the skill of the top Russian players from the time I started facing them in the World Junior Championships. I played on a line with Tony Amonte and Mike Modano, and we were matched up against the Russian super line of Alexander Mogilny, Sergei Fedorov, and Pavel Bure.

In case you are wondering, the six of us combined for 2,883 goals during our NHL careers. Modano, Amonte, and I totaled 1,490 goals. Modano led with 561, while I had 513 and Amonte netted 416. The three Russian players totaled 1,393, with Fedorov scoring 483. Mogilny came in at 473 and Bure scored 437 times.

Bure was so fucking fast that he seemed bionic. He only needed two strides to reach top speed, and he seemed to look faster with the puck than he did without it.

All six of us could skate like the wind, but if I had to handicap the field I would say Bure was fastest, followed in order by Fedorov, Amonte, Modano, me, and then Mogilny.

People used to tell me that I was a graceful skater and that I made skating look effortless, but I always felt as if I was working my ass off.

Bure, Fedorov, and Mogilny always made it seem like they were hardly working. Mogilny could ramp up to top speed without showing a bead of sweat.

Igor Larionov was another Russian I loved playing against, because he was magical with the puck.

I was in awe of these guys, jealous of their skill, because I believed they were always about to do something spectacular. I wouldn't take my eyes off them in a game. They rarely disappointed me.

Today, I enjoy watching Ovechkin because he can take over a game like he's the king of the jungle. He can dominate with his physical play and his goal-scoring ability. With the way we play defense today in the NHL, not many players can do that.

I believe we have witnessed Ovechkin mature into a player who is fully committed to winning. He still loves to have a good time at night, but he knows when it's time to go home.

At the All-Star Game in Columbus, Ovechkin hung out with my group at a bar. Late into the night, some of us ended up at a local strip club. I believe it was a member of Ovechkin's posse who came up with the idea. Truthfully, I had not been to one in years. The theory was that Columbus is a college town—the home of Ohio State—so a strip club there would be hopping and fun.

Boy, were we wrong in that assessment. We should have left the minute we walked in the door. The crowd was not entertaining. The atmosphere was not fun.

I'm not exaggerating when I tell you that a couple of women were missing teeth. The place was not what we expected.

But we ended up staying because the place had a grill and a chef who was cooking up pancakes, waffles, and chicken. It was 3:00 in the morning and we were starving.

Women kept coming up to our table, offering to provide us with lap dances, but we shooed them away.

"No offense, honey," someone said. "But these chicken and waffles are far more desirable."

And where was Ovechkin as this debauchery was going on? He was at his hotel sound asleep. He had abandoned us hours before, because he had a game the next day.

Ovechkin, in the prime of his career, realizes that it is better for him and his image if he samples the nightlife in moderation.

That's the kind of realization that didn't come to me until I was 33 or 34. Probably, my NBC producer Sam Flood, my wife, Tracy, and others might argue that the realization still hasn't come to me.

ONE

THE FATHER'S DAUGHTER

CHAPTER ONE

The Father's Daughter

My daughter, Brandi, a nationally ranked dressage rider, quit her sport and moved out of our house when she was a teenager. She told us she didn't want to go to college. She didn't want horses dictating the course of her life. Mostly, she didn't want her parents telling her what was in her best interests.

As defiant words poured from her mouth, it reminded me of the rebellious attitude I embraced after I started playing for the Chicago Blackhawks in 1988.

Like the lyrics from the Billy Joel song, Brandi had grown up just like me. She inherited her dad's stubbornness and his disdain for being told what to do. She knows it, too. Brandi has said numerous times that she is like me in many ways, and she seems to realize that is not always a good thing.

While I understood my daughter's attitude, I wasn't any less angry about her decision. Her retirement from dressage came a few months after I paid a handsome sum for a seven-year-old coal-black mare named Apassionata. This horse had been competing successfully in Germany. My daughter was a potential 2015 Pan-American Games competitor, and putting her with this world-class horse seemed like the right move.

Brandi had been very excited about the purchase of the mare. She had nicknamed her "Pia." She had traveled to Germany to train with her before the horse was brought to America.

"I am really excited for this horse and the future that we have in store together," she was quoted as saying on dressage-news.com.

She told the website that Apassionata was "eager to please and take care of her rider." At that point, Brandi sounded like someone who knew what she wanted, and maybe she did. But not all that long after giving that interview, Brandi decided she wanted to go in a different direction with her life. There was a guy involved, but she said her decision wasn't just about him.

Brandi also declared that she couldn't deal with the pressure anymore. She knew how much the horse cost, and she knew there was money riding on her performances. She knew we looked at the horse as an investment. Maybe we put too much pressure on her.

She also didn't like our rules. Tracy and I had told her that if we were going to financially support her riding career, we expected her to go to college while she was training. She didn't like our plan.

I understood how she was feeling, because there were times when I was young that I wanted to quit hockey because I believed my dad was too hard on me. I knew her feelings about the pressure were genuine. But if that was the lone issue, we could have resolved that.

Parenting is an impossible task. I love my children beyond measure, but I'm sure they have taken years off my life thanks to worrying about their futures. You hope your children grow up to be independent and strong. All parents need to let their children find their own way. You want them to have the maturity to make their own decisions. But you also feel like you have to step in when they are making poor decisions. Isn't that what parents are supposed to do?

Isn't it my job to push or inspire my child to explore all of her talents? I don't want Brandi to have regrets 20 years from now about what she did with her life. From where I'm sitting, it seems like a fine line between being an overbearing parent and a parent who wants the best for his child.

It was crushing for Tracy not to have the relationship she wanted with her daughter because of the tension brought about by Brandi's decision.

Parents strive to instill values in their children. They want their children to stick to their commitments and not quit on their dreams. On the other hand, Tracy and I understood the sacrifices that Brandi was making to compete. Having played 20 seasons in the NHL, I understand that staying on the top of your sport precludes having a normal life. Tracy understands that as well, because she disrupted her life plan to allow me to skate in the spotlight.

We understood what Brandi was giving up. Tracy would tell her to set the alarm for 5:30 every morning. They needed to be at the barn at 6:00 AM every day to feed and groom the horses. For Brandi, it was starring in *Groundhog Day*. When you are working with horses, it's the same fucking day over and over again. That can get monotonous for a 17-year-old. She wanted to see her friends, hang out with guys, and be a normal teenager.

I understood her position, but as a parent, I believed she was throwing away a golden opportunity. I know she misses the horses. One of our horses was injured after Brandi quit the sport, and we considered putting her down. The way Brandi reacted on her Facebook page made it clear to me that she still cared deeply about the sport.

No one can relate to the emotional side of being an athlete more than me. But I also understand that there were many times in my young adult life when I wouldn't listen to Tracy or others who tried to convince me that I was making poor decisions.

I was a straight arrow when I was a teenager. I did what my parents told me. I was totally focused on my goal of making it to the National Hockey League. But once I arrived in the NHL, I began to indulge my rebellious tendencies. I stayed out too late, hung out with the wrong people, and made some poor decisions. My stubborn streak rose to the surface.

Once I put on an NHL sweater, I developed an I-can-do-no-wrong attitude, and Brandi seems to have inherited that trait from me. Her attitude is, I'm right about everything. There are parallels to our lives. She has never gotten into any real trouble, either. But just as I did early in my career, Brandi likes to stay out into the wee hours of the morning. She has people in her life who aren't always the best influences. Unquestionably, I can relate to that.

Both of us were out on our own when we were teenagers, living like grown-ups, when we were not fully mature enough to handle all of that responsibility.

I've given her my share of tough love, saying words that made me cringe. Since I travel often for my NBC job, Tracy has been left to deal with most of the issues. But I've played the bad cop on more than one occasion.

Once, Brandi called me and asked, "Do we have health insurance?"

"*I* have health insurance," I told her, making my point quite succinctly.

"Sorry I asked," she said, angered by my response.

She responded the way I would have responded. I had no desire to attend college, and she says college isn't for her. I have multiple tattoos. She has multiple tattoos.

Brandi has become the rebel without a cause, just like I was. The frustration for me is that I've been where she is now, believing that I knew all I needed to know. I can explain to her, in great detail, that there are decisions you make when you are young that you later regret. But she is not in a place where she wants to listen to me. I know that place because I used to live there. Tracy and others would tell me that I was making poor decisions. But I couldn't bring myself to listen.

* * *

When I talk about that period of my life, I call it the "cuckoo crazy days." I had a lot of crazy, stupid, regrettable moments, especially in the 1990s. I didn't fully appreciate that I had issues, nor was I willing to listen to anyone who suggested I was making poor choices.

My immaturity and rebellious attitude showed in one of my first appearances at the NBC Celebrity Golf Tournament at Lake Tahoe in about 1997.

Paired up with Czech tennis star Ivan Lendl, I was nervous when we started the tournament on Friday by teeing off on No. 10. I've always been a quality golfer, but back then I wasn't a contender to win the tournament like I am today.

My putting was atrocious that day. I three-putted the first six greens. Then I four-putted my seventh hole, and followed up with two more three-putts to finish with 28 putts for nine holes.

Lendl was an avid hockey fan, a regular at Hartford Whalers games, and he seemed to take great pleasure in kidding me about my struggles with the putter.

He started calling me "Lippy" after a couple of my putts lipped out after circling the hole.

Once, I was within 12 inches of the hole and Lendl said, "Close your eyes, kid, and you'll have a better chance of making it."

He was having great fun at my expense, and I was a bubbling cauldron. For several holes, I had been ready to boil over. It finally happened on the par-five No. 18. It was my ninth hole, and I found the green with my second shot, only to three-putt for a par.

As soon as dropped my third putt into the hole, I started walking off the green. I didn't even bother to retrieve my ball.

I didn't say a word as I made my way through the gallery, and marched across the beach to the water's edge. Once I arrived there, I flung the putter as far as I could into the water. I bet it traveled 40 yards in the air.

My decision to go as close as I could to the water was based on my fear that if I tried to throw the putter into the water from the green, I would have missed the water. I had missed everything else with that putter.

It never occurred to me that my problem was pilot error. I believed it was the putter's fault. I was committed to that logic.

Anger had overrun my emotions by that point. And now I had another problem, because at that point I didn't know all the rules of golf.

I didn't know that by throwing that club into the lake, I had forfeited my right to use a putter. If it had been broken in the act of a swing, I could have replaced it. Because I had drowned that club in a fit of anger, it was considered a discarded club.

My caddie Jeff Mages offered to dive into the water in an effort to find my discarded putter, but I wouldn't let him.

"Dude, do you know how many dead bodies are lying next to my putter?" I said. "I'm not letting you dive into that."

The end result was that I had to use a driver as a putter on my final nine holes that day. Somehow, I ended up with 19 putts on my second nine, nine strokes better than I totaled on the front nine. I was still pissed off when I headed off to the local Harrah's Casino to gamble.

This was at a time in my life when I was gambling too much. Feeling shitty about the way I was golfing, I tried to console myself by taking out a $50,000 marker.

I lost the whole thing in 15 minutes. I asked for another $25,000 marker.

You can see where this is going.

Although I managed to hang on to that $25,000 for a while, I did eventually lose all of that as well.

By then it was 4:30 in the morning, and I'd been drinking heavily. I was furious at myself. There was no one else in the casino. I was scheduled to tee off at 8:00 AM. I should have cut my losses and headed to my room. But I wasn't that smart on that day.

I thought, *Fuck it. I'm going to take out another $50,000 marker.*

That was probably the dumbest decision I had made since I squared off against 220-pound Los Angeles Kings defenseman Marty McSorley for my first NHL fight during the 1989–90 season. What the hell was I thinking when I hit McSorley with that check? And what the hell was I thinking when I concluded that more gambling was in my best interest?

Taking another $50,000 that night should have been an indication that my gambling could cause me serious problems. In the past, I wagered more conservatively and could have made a $25,000 marker last all night. I had never before been this aggressive at the tables.

Now down $75,000, I took my $50,000 marker and went to the VIP room, where I played blackjack at $10,000 per hand, three hands at a time.

I started at 19 on my first hand, had a pair of threes on my second hand, and a seven and four for 11 on my third hand. I split the threes. On my first three, I drew an eight, to give me 11. But at that point I was out of money, so I had to take out another $10,000 marker. My next card was an eight, giving me 19 on that hand.

On the second of my two threes, I drew a 10, then pulled a four to give me 17 on that hand.

Now I was sitting with 19, 19, and 17 on my first three hands. I double-downed on my last hand and drew a nine to give me 20.

I had $60,000 at stake on the table, but my four hands were all potential winners. The dealer had two sevens. I was feeling confident.

I was smashed—embarrassingly drunk—and I was screaming at the dealer to pull a face card. I needed her to bust. You probably could have heard me in the next county.

Instead, the dealer drew another seven for 21.

Could there be anything worse that getting beat by three sevens?

My total loss was $135,000. I don't ever remember being angrier than I was at that moment.

The dealer shuffled the decks of cards while I sat on my stool, stewing. She handed me the yellow card to cut the deck for the shoe. Instead of sliding in the yellow card into the deck, I grabbed the entire deck and hurled it toward her. Cards exploded in every direction.

Then I picked up the chair I was sitting on and hurled it across the casino. I actually considered turning over the table but opted to walk out instead.

I had just enough time to pull myself together and play my round of golf. I shot an 85, and then I headed back to the casino.

As I walked in, there were three extra-large guys dressed in expensive suits standing there waiting for me. It looked like a scene from the movie *Casino*.

"Mr. Roenick," one of them said. "We'd like to have a word with you."

They lead me to the back of casino, asked me to sit down, and rolled the video of what had transpired the night before.

"We don't tolerate this kind of behavior, and we are banning you for the rest of your trip here," one guy said.

Tournament organizers also found out what I had done at the casino and banned me for one year.

I really didn't cause any monetary damage. Basically, I was banned for being a total dick. I was incredibly apologetic because I knew my behavior was three steps beyond unacceptable. My bad karma from the golf course had followed me to the casino, and I should have seen that happening.

Sometimes, it seems as if karma is the determining factor in gambling. Once, I was hanging out with a celebrity buddy at a casino and he took out $750,000 in markers and lost every dollar. He asked for another $250,000 marker, then gave $100,000 to each of the two dealers who had been at his table. That's right—this guy gave two casino employees $100,000 tips. (I will protect his identity because I believe he doesn't want his gambling habits publicized.)

Now holding only $50,000, he resumed gambling and won his $1 million back, and then some. Anyone who watched that performance came away believing in good karma.

Once, I felt the karma changing for me when I was gambling at Caesars Palace in Las Vegas. Every hand seemed to be going the dealer's way. I had 20, and he hit an eight for 21. I had an 18, and he drew 19. I would take a hit on 12 and bust. It was a frustrating night. Already down $70,000, I asked for another $10,000 marker. Within minutes, I had lost $9,500 of that money. The run of bad luck I was having seemed unprecedented.

I sat there holding my final $500 chip. The dealer looked impatient as I contemplated my losses. He seemed to be staring right through me. It made me want to reach across the table and rip his head off.

But the rage suddenly just went away, and I turned to a friend and said, "Well, if you have a chip, you have a chance."

I placed the $500 bet and won. Then I pressed that bet, and won again. Now I had $2,000, and I bet that amount and won. Then I bet $1,000. I won. Now sitting there with $5,000, I could feel the luck turning. "Fuck it," I said. "I've come this far, let's see if I can win again."

My bet was $5,000 and I won again. Thirty minutes later, I was sitting with $120,000 in chips in front of me. I paid off my markers and then got the fuck out of Dodge. When you magically transform a $500 chip into $100,000, it's time to take your winnings and call it a night. A date with good karma is always a one-night stand. Good karma lays with you for a short time and then she leaves. You don't know when she will be back. Karma can be a bitch.

My Harrah's Casino explosion did not have any long-term consequences. I return to that casino every year, and I am welcomed. Some of the long-time employees remember that night or have heard the story. One of the older guys there always says to me, "We are going to have a good trip this year, aren't we, Mr. Roenick?"

Although I've never had any trouble in a casino since that night, I've always managed to find different levels of trouble at the Lake Tahoe tournament. That's been a problem because I now work for NBC. Every year, Sam Flood, NBC's executive producer, gives me a speech about not causing any problems in Tahoe.

And damn if I don't let it happen every year.

Just a few years ago, I was playing in the tournament and having a good round heading into the 18th hole.

Unfortunately, I flubbed my tee shot into the hazard, landing my ball just to the right of the cart path. It was near the beach, meaning it was a sandy area. But the real issue was all of the television cables that were snaking around in support of NBC's coverage of the event.

The cables were inside the hazard line, and my ball was nestled between them. The rules say you can move the ball if you are impeded by an unnatural object. But I was in the hazard. Seeing it as a gray area, I asked for a ruling.

Cameras were rolling when the rules official came over and informed me that because of the cables, I would be allowed to take a drop within two club lengths without a penalty.

"Are you sure?" I asked.

"Yes," he said.

Satisfied, I took the drop, and ended up recording a bogey-six on the par-5 hole. I considered that a good result, given where my tee shot landed.

The celebrity tournament is played under the Stableford scoring system, and a bogey didn't cost me any points. For this 54-hole celebrity event, a par is one point, a birdie is three points, an eagle is six points, and a double eagle is 10 points. A hole in one is eight points. A bogey is no points. A double-bogey is minus-two. The player with the highest point total wins the event. The difference between a bogey and a double-bogey was significant to me.

When I went in to the scorer's tent to verify my total, the scorer had me down as recording a seven on that 18th hole. I pointed out that I actually had a six.

"No," he said. "We gave you a penalty stroke on that hole."

"But I asked for a ruling, and the scorer said I could drop without a penalty," I insisted.

An argument ensued. It escalated quickly. As we all know, I'm a competitive son of a gun. And I wasn't going to accept a minus-two without a fight, especially when I believed I was being wronged.

Finally, the man who had made the ruling on the course was summoned, and he denied telling me that I had a free drop. It didn't take long for my temper to boil over at everyone in my vicinity. My language went further out of bounds than my tee shot had. I verbally abused the man who had given me the incorrect information.

Nobody from NBC believed I had acted appropriately, but some of the workers reviewed the tapes and said that the scorer did indeed tell me that I could have a free drop. But that didn't matter. NBC officials told me to apologize to the man. NBC analyst Johnny Miller said I needed to apologize. And I did.

Sam Flood asked me again to tone down my act, and I had every intention of doing that. But in 2014, I had some friends following me on the course, and one of them, Rich Turasky, is a guy who likes to razz me non-stop.

He was needling me the entire day, and late in the round, while I was contending for the championship, Turasky was giving me the business about landing in a bunker at a key time in the match.

"You will never get up and down from there," he crowed. "You have no hope."

Digging in with my cleats, I lofted the ball out of the trap with one of the best shots of the round. Considering the trash talking that was being heaped on me, I was rather proud of that up-and-down.

But as I marched up the next fairway, Rich wouldn't give me credit for hitting that spectacular shot. Retired LPGA star Annika

Sorenstam was in the field with us, and Rich pointed out that Annika had stuck it closer.

Fed up, I gave him a middle-finger salute. Unfortunately, I didn't see the NBC camera tracking me. The network captured the moment on live TV.

My phone rang shortly thereafter. It was Sam Flood.

As a father who doesn't always agree with everything his children do, I think I know just how he felt.

TWO

WHAT THEY DON'T TELL YOU

CHAPTER TWO

What They Don't Tell You

When I was an emerging prep school hockey star at Thayer Academy in Braintree, Massachusetts, in the 1980s, my dream wasn't to pay income tax in 22 states or to have my own stalker. I didn't long for the day when being offered risky investment options would seem like a daily occurrence. I didn't wish to be so famous that a troll on Twitter would say publicly that he hoped my children died in a fiery automobile crash.

I just dreamed of playing in the NHL. The rest of it was just a "bonus."

While I was busy hoping to have an Olympic moment as wondrous as the one Mike Eruzione had in Lake Placid, it never occurred to me that there are aspects of stardom that will fuck up your life if you let them. I've never for a second wished I wasn't a NHL star. But it is not all glamour and glory. I wish that I would have handled the trappings of stardom better than I did. Tracy and I can testify to the fact that playing in the NHL brings some misery to accompany the blessings.

I would bet there is a moment in every player's career, even if it only lasts for a second, when things seem overwhelming. When I was a young player, everyone advised me on how to be ready to compete as a player. They told me how to improve my strength, my speed, and my agility. They told me how to lengthen my stride and increase the velocity of my shot. But no one told me how to react when a screaming Mike Keenan put his hands around my throat.

At 18, I was playing my second NHL exhibition game, against the Minnesota North Stars, in Kalamazoo, Michigan, when Keenan became enraged that I didn't finish a check. He stalked me from behind the bench, then put his hands around my neck and pulled me back so he could look me in the eyes, and said, "If you pass up one more fucking hit in this fucking game, you will never play another fucking game in this league."

Those words will remain deposited in my memory bank until my dying breath.

Before I was drafted, I was thinking about what it might be like to score a game-winning goal, not what it would be like to have a maniacal coach assault me during a game. I dreamed of flying down the ice at Mach 2, with my jersey flapping behind me, not feeling as if I had the weight of an entire city on my shoulders if I wasn't playing well. I loved the fame and wealth that came with being a NHL player, but I now recognize that my fame came with a price. I paid that price in full by hurting people who matter to me.

When you become a professional athlete, you enter a wonderful place primarily full of cheerful fans who want to celebrate your ability. They want to cheer you, shake your hand, and get your signature on a piece of paper. They want to stand next to you and have their photograph snapped. That's an enjoyable aspect of pro sports. Any athlete who says he doesn't enjoy having countless numbers of fans adore him isn't being truthful.

However, there is another side of pro sports that isn't as fun. You learn quickly that there are trolls on social media who strive to make you miserable. There are con artists looking to steal your future. There are well-meaning people who try to lure you into business deals that are not in your best interest. There are bad people who want to take you down any way they can, sometimes out of envy, sometimes out of greed.

Today, the NHL Players' Association and the NHL have a fall orientation seminar for young players to help them prepare to deal with the issues outside the game, like tax responsibilities, investment schemes, and the like. But when I entered the league, we mostly had to avoid the landmines on our own. Many of us were blown up a few times in the process. In fairness, my agent, Neil Abbott, did counsel me on going into an NHL career with my eyes wide open. Because of his guidance, I have money set aside for retirement.

When you are about to turn pro, here are just some of the things they don't tell you:

Your body is a war zone.

When I joined the Chicago Blackhawks in 1988, I was thinking about making plays, scoring goals, and winning games. I wasn't thinking about how physically demanding it is to be a pro athlete.

Nobody warns you about the physical toll that will be extracted from you each time you play a game. I lost between five and eight pounds of water weight every time I played a game in the NHL. Obviously I was used to playing the game at a high level, but nothing prepares you for professional sports.

When you wake up after a game, your body feels depleted. You are sore. Players are skating around at close to 30 miles per hour, and the average player now seems to be about 6-foot-2, 210 pounds. Each check has the impact of an automobile crash, and that's what it feels like the morning after every game. You didn't break any bones, but you were knocked around a bit when the airbags deployed. You are achy, and your joints and muscles rebel against the notion that they are scheduled to work today.

I experienced that feeling 1,363 times in my career, having played 524 games with the Chicago Blackhawks, 454 with the Phoenix Coyotes, 216 with the Philadelphia Flyers, 111 with the San Jose Sharks, and 58 with the Los Angeles Kings. I also played in 154 playoff games, where the intensity level is even higher.

Only six years out of the game, I have already had left knee surgery to repair the wear and tear I had from my playing career. I needed my meniscus repaired. Plus, I had a micro-fracture. My knee just gave out one day. To be honest, this was my fault, for not continuing to work out the way I should have after I retired. When you retire, the tendency is not to be as vigilant watching your weight.

I had gained too many pounds. When I appeared on television playing in the Celebrity Golf Tournament in 2014, the running joke was that I must have eaten my caddie.

Still, it seems like I'm luckier than most retired players. I have some issues regarding the rotation of my shoulder. I had shoulder surgery when I was playing. But mostly I've left the game in decent shape. I've never, for example, had any back issues.

As this book was being written, it was revealed that former NHL defenseman Steve Montador died of what was said to be "natural causes." But we all know there is nothing natural about someone dying at age 35.

Montador had played 571 NHL games, and then had been forced to retire because of lingering concussion issues. His former Chicago Blackhawks teammate Dan Carcillo was quoted in media stories saying Montador suffered from bouts of depression after he left the game. Plus, Carcillo noted that he had noticed a "deterioration" of Montador's mental state over the last few years of his life.

Understanding that he was experiencing problems, Montador signed up to have his brain studied after his death. When that autopsy was completed, it showed that he suffered from widespread Chronic Traumatic Encephalopathy (CTE), a degenerative brain disorder linked to repeated blows to the head. Through autopsy findings, it has been revealed in recent years that several former NFL and NHL players have suffered from CTE. Other deceased NHL players who showed signs of CTE include Bob Probert, who I knew well, plus Rick Martin, Reg Fleming, and Derek Boogaard.

CTE can only be diagnosed posthumously, but doctors might suspect the presence of CTE in the living when they see symptoms such as memory loss, depression, or loss of impulse control. Some former players who were discovered to have CTE had showed signs of progressive dementia before their death.

The discussion over CTE and the long-term impact of multiple concussions concerns me because I believe I suffered 13 or 14 concussions in my career. I've started to notice that my memory isn't as sharp as I want it to be. I struggle to come up with names of people I should know. I seem to have lapses. Is that the normal aging process or is the early stages of possible dementia? The question has crossed my mind.

During my career, my head suffered major trauma. The scariest moment came when Boris Mironov's rocket-launcher slap shot blew apart my face, causing 21 official breaks. The surgery to repair that damage came roughly five years after the surgery to repair the jaw damage I suffered when mammoth defenseman Derian Hatcher hit me.

The hardest hit I ever endured was from defenseman Jim Johnson, back when he was playing for the Minnesota North Stars. It was an inadvertent elbow right to my chin. I woke up 20 minutes later lying on the training table. I had no idea how I had gotten there.

Another time, I was decked by former St. Louis Blues forward Geoff Courtnall after I had scored a beautiful top-shelf goal. He put me in the hospital for the night.

Those hits caused two of my concussions. Could the accumulation of all of those hits cause me major issues down the road? I don't have an answer for that.

However, I've recently decided that I would like to have my brain studied after my death. Given the number of hits my body absorbed, and the number of concussions I believe I suffered, I suspect they might find evidence of CTE. At the very least, I suspect my brain would have some value to those studying the impact playing in the NHL or NFL has on the brain.

It would be an exaggeration to say that I'm worried about this issue. I don't worry about much in my life. I see worrying as a waste of time and energy. I feel like whatever is going to happen is going to happen. I try to do the best I can for my body and then I let nature take its course.

Knowing everything I know about concussions now, would I change the way I played? Absolutely not.

Today's players are better conditioned than my generation was. Their training habits are improved, but I guarantee you that the players arriving in today's game still are surprised how much their bodies are beat up by playing in the NHL. Regardless of how well conditioned you are, your body is damaged when New York Islanders forward Matt Martin staples you to the boards.

A Mercedes is a well-engineered, durable automobile, but it still suffers damage when it is involved in a head-on collision. Imagine what a Mercedes would look like if it was involved in one accident, or multiple accidents, on 1,363 different days? That's essentially what happens with players. That's why experts are studying our brains after we're gone.

Pressure can be debilitating.

The physical exertion is less than half of the challenge for NHL players. The mental pressure that athletes face today can be overwhelming, especially with social media now playing such a prominent role in our lives.

The life of an NHL player, particularly a top player, is a roller coaster ride. Expectations are always high. Team management has expectations. Coaches have expectations. You have your own expectations. The media can be an ally when your performance level is high, but if you are struggling, the media pressure feels crushing.

Coaches' futures depend on how you play and they are constantly on you about what you are doing on the ice.

Most workers in North America receive performance reviews once a year. NHL players receive performance reviews after all 82 regular-season games and every playoff game.

Nothing happens on the ice that isn't scrutinized by the coaches, the media, and now by fans online.

Sometimes it feels like there is no breathing room. The pressure can be suffocating for some players. Those who allow the pressure to get to them feel like they are in a prison surrounded by guard towers. It feels like there is no way out, and the spotlight always finds them.

Social media is great for sharing information and starting a conversation. It can be fun for an athlete to connect with the fan base. But social media has also made life worse for athletes in a lot of ways. It has made privacy impossible. It also allows for anonymity, and fans now have the right to say exactly what they are feeling about you at any given time of the day or night.

While most fans are respectful, plenty are not. The web can be an ugly place. Verbal daggers are often thrown your way. People can rip you apart with absolutely no consequences.

Athletes today know that if they don't play well in a game, somebody out there will send them a message suggesting that the world would be a better place if they weren't in it. If an athlete makes a blunder during an important game, he knows he will face personal attacks, or even death threats, in the postgame social-media analysis of the game.

It's impossible for me to sum up how stressful social media can be for someone in the public eye. Even if you don't read what is said, you know your friends and family are reading it.

It's sad, really, because being on Twitter can be a rewarding experience. An athlete can build his brand on Twitter and let people see his personality. It's a great place to let fans know when you are doing something cool for charity.

But even if I promote a charity to help fight a disease, I guarantee you that there will be people on Twitter who will say they hope I contract that disease.

As an NBC analyst, I have been called every ugly name there is. I've also had people tell me they hope I end up in a wheelchair and that my children die in a car accident.

I've found myself in trouble regularly at NBC because I have reacted to what has been said to me on Twitter. That's one reason why I don't participate much anymore. The trolls and haters are always out there, always looking for any opportunity to spread misery. You have to wonder how sad these people's lives are that they gain pleasure from demeaning others.

I fully understand why former NBA star Charles Barkley has never had any involvement on Twitter. His position: why should he give his critics, or "knuckleheads," a place to direct their attacks?

If I was playing today, I wouldn't go anywhere near Twitter; I would let my play do the talking. That may be hard for people to believe, given my personality. I like to dance in the middle of the dancefloor. But social media is a scary place. I have to hang out there because I'm on television. But athletes don't have to be.

Fandom can get too personal.

When I played in the NHL, I had fans who sometimes followed me from city to city. Most of them were passionate hockey fans who simply liked my personality or the way I played. They would be happy if I acknowledged them or stopped to say hello or posed for a photograph. But occasionally, athletes end up with fans who cross the line.

When I was playing for the Phoenix Coyotes, I ended up with a female fan who became such a problem that I had to ask NHL security for help.

Because I lived in a gated community, this woman couldn't get close to my house. But she would park outside the gates, wait for me to leave, and then follow me. Her office was filled with photos of me that she took with her personal camera; she posted about them often on her website. Then at some point it started to feel like she wanted to ruin my life. She started to dig into my personal life, acquiring information about my friends and spreading lies about me.

She would show up at places she knew I would be and make inappropriate comments. She once said, "I don't what you see in Tracy. She may be prettier than me, but I have better boobs than her."

"Get the fuck away from me," I would say, but she would keep showing up.

It was difficult to build a stalking case against her because she would follow me to public places and would have a reason to be there. I confronted her once at a public ice rink when my son, Brett, was playing, but she said she was there because her daughter was playing.

This went on for 10 years, even after I left the Coyotes but was still living in Arizona. For a while we received threatening letters— unsigned, of course. We always suspected the letters were from her but we never had any proof.

The woman had crushes on other Coyotes players as well, but I seemed to be her main target. It finally stopped but there was considerable misery associated with it.

When I played in the NHL I seemed to be popular with 21- to 25-year-old women. That may sound like every man's fantasy but it isn't really, not when you are married with a family. The vast majority of fans understand boundaries. They just want to support you. I always appreciated them. But there were a few fans who had no limits on what they would do.

Now that I'm retired, it's all different. I don't have younger women following me around. Now, I'm on television and my fans are 50- to 65-year-old women. All they want from me is to stop and pose for a photograph with them. I'm happy to oblige.

Your money is only partially yours.

Your tax rate is going to be around 40 percent, and it could be higher depending upon which state you live in. It costs you more to live in California and less to live in Florida.

The more money you have, the harder it can be to hold on to. You must pay taxes in every state where you make money. In other words, when you play for the Chicago Blackhawks and take a road trip to play the Los Angeles Kings and Anaheim, you are obligated to pay California taxes.

Top NHL players make millions of dollars in a short period of time, and for some of them it's enough to support them the rest of their lives. For others, it is not. I played with guys who lived lavishly and I played with guys who probably still have their per diem money from their days on the road in the 1990s.

I didn't live frugally. I traveled. I gambled. I ate at expensive restaurants. I spent too much money. When I retired, I probably had about 25 percent of my earnings; fortunately for me, Abbott had encouraged me to put some of my money into safe, long-term investments to insure that I will have enough money in my golden years.

If a rookie asked me today what percent of his money he should have when he retires, I would say 35 or 40 percent. You should live well when you are playing because you are earning that money. A player isn't any different than an average American. Lots of us buy more house than we need and more expensive cars than we need. But there's no reason a guy's playing career shouldn't leave him enough money to live on for the rest of his life.

Learn to say "No."

Over 20 NHL seasons, I scored 513 goals and probably rejected 513 investment opportunities.

Because athletes have large incomes, they are bombarded by friends, family members, and acquaintances presenting investment opportunities that range from reasonable to the truly hair-brained.

It was so hard for me to say "no" to family members that I actually employed people to do it for me. Most times when I got a request, I would say, "You'll have to talk to my accountant."

There are plenty of horror stories out there about guys who lost hundreds of thousands or even millions of dollars in investments that were too good to be true. While writing this book, I was reading about a trial being held in Central Islip, Long Island, for Tommy Constantine and Phil Kenner, who were convicted of cheating more than a dozen NHL players out of at least $30 million. (That verdict may be challenged by their defense.)

Constantine was my neighbor in Arizona and was constantly asking me to invest in golf courses located in Mexico. I just never had a good feeling about the situation, and declined the opportunity repeatedly.

I read about that trial and thought, *That could have been me.*

I've had my fair share of both good and bad investments. Someone approached me about investing $25,000 in a piece of property that he hoped to develop for the Caterpillar Company. It seemed like he had a reasonable strategy, and I agreed to give him my money. Eighteen months later, my share of the sale of property was worth $380,000.

My advice to all athletes is that when you are approached to invest in a restaurant or bar, run or skate away as fast you can. Restaurants and bars always seem like a good idea because you believe that your popularity will translate into people going to your restaurant. It doesn't seem to work that way, although my friend, Chris Chelios, seems to have made it work in both Chicago and Detroit.

An Italian restaurant didn't pay off for me. I invested $300,000 in a pizza restaurant in Phoenix, and I was left with nothing to show for it when it shut down. When I invested my money, I believed I was investing in a chain. But when the Phoenix restaurant closed, I was told that I had invested in that particular location only. I was told that restaurant was dead, so my money was gone.

"What about all of the equipment that was in the restaurant?" I asked.

I was told that the pots, pans, stoves, kitchen utensils, and everything else was going to a new location that was being opened. My contention was that I owned a percentage of those items so I should get a percentage of ownership in the new restaurant.

Originally, my former partners didn't see it that way. But eventually I did end up with a 5 percent ownership stake. So how much wealth have I accumulated as a result of that 5 percent? Not a cent.

Like I said, run if you are asked to invest in a restaurant.

Land and real estate deals have paid off the best for me. I bought my wife's horse barn and property for $1.5 million and seven years later sold it for $3.8 million.

As a rule, I prefer safer investments. If I can earn 5 or 6 percent through investing in a government bond, I'm very happy. But I also enjoy gambling a bit, which explains why I bought the German horse. We bought her for my daughter to ride in competition, but we also are hoping the horse can become a champion and see her value rise significantly. If she performs the way my wife believes she can, then our investment could turn into a nice profit.

When Brandi retired from the sport, our investment wasn't looking good. But when one door closes, another opens, and Tracy decided to climb back in the saddle and compete. She had stopped competing to help Brandi develop her career, but with Brandi now out, Tracy decided to compete with our horse. Although she had been out of competition since 2005, she has done very well.

It's still unknown whether our horse investment will pay off. It's crazy when you think about it—we have a pile of cash riding on a horse's ability to learn a few dance moves. That's really what it comes down to.

As you might imagine, it's always hard to say "no" to people you care about. Thankfully, sometimes you can find a win-win situation, such as the golf course I bought in Pembroke, Massachusetts, a few years ago. My parents are running it and it's become a part of the community. I feel like I'm helping them take care of themselves, and the course is very successful with lots of great members. Sometimes what's good for the soul is also good for the bottom line.

It's never easy to be traded.

As a player, you always know in the back of your mind that trades are just a part of sports, but it's still shocking when it happens to you or a close teammate. It felt like a catastrophic loss when the Chicago Blackhawks traded Bryan Marchment in 1993. Tracy was tight with Bryan's wife, Kim, and Bryan and I were inseparable. We actually broke down and cried when we got the news.

Bryan and I don't talk much now, but when we do it's as if we never spent time apart. We pick up right where we left off when the trade happened.

Even though I knew that I was going to be dealt by the Blackhawks in 1996, it was still a shock when they pulled the trigger on the deal that sent me to the Phoenix Coyotes for Alexei Zhamnov, Craig Mills, and a first-round draft pick.

I had been thinking that I was going to end up with the New York Islanders. Mike Milbury, my NBC partner today, was the Islanders' general manager then. He has told me that he carried around an offer sheet for about 10 days while he was trying to negotiate a deal with the Blackhawks. How would things for me and the Islanders franchise changed if I had gone there?

But all trades are hurtful, regardless of where you are headed. When a team trades you, it means the team's management doesn't want you anymore. That's not easy to accept. You can choose to be either hurt or angry, but either way it's unpleasant. Then there are the practical aspects. Just imagine for a few seconds what it would be like if you were told right this second that you had been traded to a new company. You have to report to your new employer tomorrow, likely in another state, and start work immediately. Your family is left to pick up the pieces of your life. You say good-bye to close friends, knowing you might not see them for months, if ever again.

And you are never prepared for all of the trade rumors that routinely pop up. It's worse today because social media allows a rumor to circle the globe in seconds. In 1927, it was monumental news that Charles Lindbergh could fly from Garden City, New York, to Paris in 33 hours and 30 minutes. Today, if Florida Panthers right wing Jaromir Jagr farts during a game in Sunrise, Florida, fans in his native Czech Republic will read about it on Twitter before the smell dissipates.

The rumor that bothered me the most came before the 1991–92 season, when there were league-wide rumblings that the Blackhawks were willing to trade me to the Quebec Nordiques in a deal to secure the rights to Eric Lindros, who had refused to report to the team after being picked first overall in the 1991 draft.

Chicago general manager Mike Keenan was clearly fascinated by Lindros, who was being cast as a modern-day Gordie Howe. He was 240 pounds and could pulverize opponents with high megaton hits on one end of the ice, then humble goalies with his considerable skill.

When Keenan picked Lindros to play in the 1991 Canada Cup and Lindros played impressively, it simply gave stronger legs to the Lindros-to-Chicago rumor.

At the time, my agent was trying to negotiate a new contract with the Blackhawks. I was 21, coming off a 41-goal season, and Abbott was telling me that we might be able to secure a long-term deal that would set me up for life. Then suddenly I was hearing and reading that there was a possibility that I might be shipped to Quebec City.

The rumor was strong enough that Abbott cut off negotiations until he was given assurances that I wouldn't be traded. The rumor had several different versions, but the popular one was the Blackhawks sending me, defenseman Dave Manson, and goaltender Jimmy Waite to the Nordiques for Lindros. Based on what Quebec eventually received for Lindros' rights, we can guess that there could have been a first-round pick included in that offer, if it was truly made.

"The Hawks have denied there's anything to it," Abbott told the *Chicago Tribune*. "But the rumors continue and I hear from different sources that the Hawks and Quebec are having discussions. I think the Hawks feel strongly about Jeremy, but if the right deal comes along...well, I'm sure the league doesn't want Lindros to sit out the season."

While this was going on, I was playing for the USA in the World Cup. It was stressful to believe that the Blackhawks were considering trading me for a guy who hadn't yet played in the league. Hadn't I proven my value? Plus, the speculation was that Lindros wanted a record-breaking contract. It was reported that he wanted $3 million or more per season. I was insulted that they were considering going after a player who was going to ask for the moon before he played in the show, while telling my agent they couldn't afford to pay me $1 million per season.

We wanted a three- or four-year deal worth just over $1 million per season, and the Blackhawks were offering a four-year deal worth $3.2 million. Had we not reached an agreement, I would have earned $130,000 while playing out my option season in 1991–92.

At that time, the league's most valuable player, Mark Messier, was only making $1.5 million, and only Wayne Gretzky and Mario Lemieux were making more. Lemieux was making a shade above $2 million and Gretzky was at $3 million.

When I finally signed a five-year contract worth an average of $1 million per season, the Blackhawks said they had no desire to trade me. The word around the league was that the Blackhawks told the Nordiques they could have anyone on their roster except Chelios and me.

But even after I signed the contract, the rumor didn't fully die. Lindros refused to sign with Quebec, and ended up playing for the Canadian Olympic team. In March, *Tribune* reporter Mike Kiley wrote that while the Blackhawks were still interested in Lindros, it was unlikely I would be included in any package.

Still, Kiley included a quote from an NHL source who said that he could see a scenario where I might welcome a trade to Quebec. "Say you go to Roenick and tell him Quebec has promised to pay him $2 million a year if he'll agree to being traded for Lindros," the source told Kiley. "He'd be on the next plane out."

The truth was I wanted to stay in Chicago. I had no interest in leaving. But to be completely honest, that source was probably right. My agent and I had talked often about landing the kind of contract that would set me up for life. If the Nordiques would have given me $2 million per season, I probably could have been persuaded to head north. I was glad when Lindros was finally traded to the Philadelphia Flyers for a bushel of talent. He ended up receiving a six-year contract worth $20 million.

Given how hard the Blackhawks fought me over $200,000 per season, I just couldn't see owner Bill Wirtz agreeing to pay that amount for a player who hadn't yet played an NHL game.

When you are dreaming of playing in the NHL, you never think about the possibility that someday a team may not want you anymore. That's never part of the dream. It's just something you have to learn to accept in this line of work.

THREE

LUCKY OR GOOD?

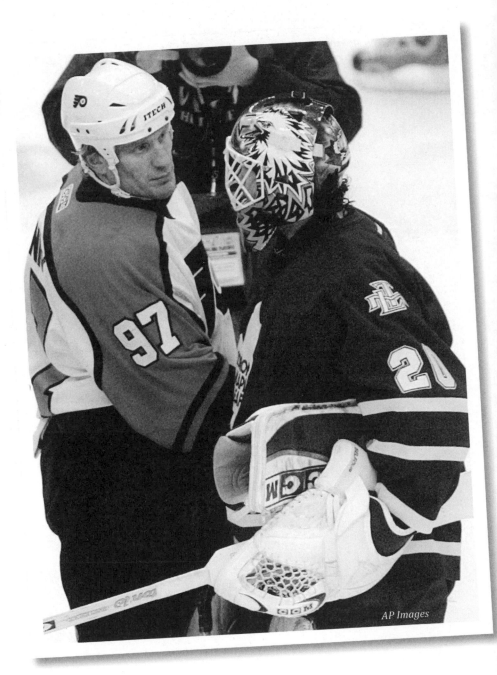

CHAPTER THREE

Lucky or Good?

One of the most spectacular goals of my NHL career was scored because human beings have an innate sense of self-preservation.

History has recorded that I scored my first professional playoff overtime goal on May 20, 1992, to give the Chicago Blackhawks a 4–3 win against the Edmonton Oilers in Game 3 of the Campbell Conference Final.

What history hasn't noted is that I scored that beautiful goal simply because I was trying to avoid being struck in the ankle by a sizzling Chris Chelios slap shot.

The *Chicago Tribune* story by Mike Kiley stated that I scored at 2:45 of overtime at Edmonton's Northlands Coliseum after taking a "pass" in the slot from Chelios.

The truth is that Chelios unleashed a screaming shot that was zeroing in on my ankle when I took a desperate, wild-ass golf swing at the puck in the hope of preventing it from breaking my ankle. I was simply trying to protect myself.

As it turned out, I made perfect contact and ripped the puck over Oilers goalie Bill Ranford for the game-winner. It clanged off the bar and dropped over the goal line. It was a top-shelf beauty.

On video, the goal made it seem as if I was the most skilled player in the NHL. The swing was perfectly timed and the shot was perfectly placed into the upper corner. On video, it was dazzling.

But the truth is that I was lucky as hell.

Anyone who played with or against Chelios knows that trying to avoid being hit by one of his slap shots is a forgivable offense. There's a difference between a hard shot and a heavy shot. A hard shot arrives in a hurry, but it doesn't cause the same level of pain as a heavy shot. All shots hurt, but a heavy shot hurts longer.

Chelios had a heavy shot. I had been struck by those often enough to know the pain stuck with you for a couple of days.

I never told anyone except Chelios that my first overtime goal was a complete fluke. Even my other teammates thought I had scored a brilliant goal. When you watch the video, it looks as if I knew exactly what I was doing.

It was an important goal because it gave us a 3–0 lead in that series. Plus, it was our 10th playoff win in a row.

This goal is evidence of the dirty little secret that no one ever talks about in sports: luck plays a much bigger role in the outcomes than we choose to admit. You certainly don't win a Stanley Cup because you are lucky, but you probably can't win one if you're not.

How many important games have been won on a goal that was as lucky as the one I scored in 1992? A lot of memorable overtime games have been decided by deflections that could just as easily have missed the net as flown into it.

Luck has always played a role in injuries, and injuries usually play a role in which team raises the Stanley Cup at the end of the year. Injuries often come down to players being in the wrong place at the wrong time. Why was I in the path of Dmitri Mironov's slap shot that shattered my jaw in 2004? If I arrived at that spot two seconds earlier or later, the puck wouldn't have touched me.

I often think about how lucky I was to avoid another broken jaw—not to mention trouble with management—when my Phoenix Coyotes teammate Rick Tocchet missed me with a right hook after I tried to pull off a practical joke against him.

One day I came up with the idea of hiding in my teammates' lockers and then jumping out to scare them. I tried it first with goaltender Nikolai Khabibulin and he turned out to be the ideal victim. When Khabibulin opened his locker, I lunged out. He shrieked like he was a doomed character in a horror move.

The encounter with Tocchet was less entertaining.

As a tough guy who sometimes let his fists do his talking, Tocchet's default reaction when someone jumped out at him from his locker was to take a wild swing that just missed connecting with my face. This failed prank happened only a couple of hours before a scheduled home game against the Detroit Red Wings.

In retrospect, I was quite fortunate that Tocchet didn't knock my block off. Had he hit me, the force of the blow would have undoubtedly knocked me out cold. There's no way I would have been able to play that night. Would the Coyotes have suspended me and Tocchet?

I was lucky that night. I was also lucky on another one of my memorable overtime goals. In 1994, Tony Amonte made a nice pass to me that struck Toronto Maple Leafs defenseman Dave Ellett's skate and deflected right onto my stick. I buried the shot top shelf past goalie Felix Potvin at 1:23 of overtime to give the Blackhawks an emotional 4–3 win.

After I scored, I skated down the ice and slid on my knees as the Chicago Stadium crowd went crazy.

This was a big win because it tied the best-of-seven series 2–2 and that guaranteed that another game would be played in Chicago Stadium. The Blackhawks were scheduled to move into the United Center the following season, and the crowd wasn't ready to say good-bye to Chicago Stadium just yet.

But here's the rest of the story: everyone concentrated so much on seeing another game at Chicago Stadium that no one gave any thought to the possibility that we might not score in the next home game.

Unfortunately, that's what happened: we were shut out in Game 5 in Toronto and lost 1–0 in Game 6 in Chicago to lose the series. That meant my overtime goal in Game 4 is the last goal ever scored at Chicago Stadium.

A photographer snapped a great photo of that tally, and I bet I've signed more than 25,000 copies of that photo in the years since. I hope the photographer was paid handsomely for that photo. If he had royalty rights, he made plenty of money.

The only other photo I've signed as often is the one snapped after I scored the overtime winner for the Philadelphia Flyers during a series-clinching game in Toronto in 2004. That was a case of making your own luck.

All of the air went out of the Air Canada Centre after that goal, which makes it one of the most memorable of my career. It was eerie. Moments before, the building was boastfully loud after Darcy

Tucker had leveled my teammate Sami Kapanen with a devastating hit. It was as if Kapanen had been trampled by a bull. Dazed and hurting, he struggled to the bench. Our teammate Keith Primeau used his stick to pull Kapanen the final few feet.

Kapanen's effort to get to the bench was one of the most impressive athletic feats I've ever witnessed. As soon as he touched the bench, I jumped on the ice like a swimmer leaving the blocks on the second leg of a relay.

Before the overtime began, I had leaned back in the dressing room and visualized what might happen. I saw myself on a 2-on-1 break.

Imagine how stunned I was when I found myself on a 2-on-1 break with my old friend Tony Amonte.

On odd man rushes, I had been passing too often. Coaches were trying to persuade me to shoot more. I knew I wasn't going to pass that night. I had visualized myself scoring the goal.

Ed Belfour was the Toronto goalie, and I knew him well from our days together in Chicago. He was one of the most competitive teammates I had ever known.

For many years in Blackhawks practices, I always tried to beat Belfour on the long side, over his right pad. That was my go-to move. Belfour knew I had scored many goals in my career with that move. Figuring Belfour was expecting it, I opted to go top shelf on the short side. It was a wise decision.

It turned out to be one of the best shots of my career. Belfour never gave a shooter much room up there, but I managed to thread the needle against him to win the game 3–2. The shot was perfect.

If I had put it an inch higher or lower, I would have missed. It was a beautiful goal to end the series.

When it happened, I was simply relieved the series was over and happy to be in the Eastern Conference Finals. I never would have guessed that Leafs fans wouldn't see another playoff game for nine years.

The photo was great because you could see Toronto fans with their faces buried in their hands, or the mouths hanging wide open. In the background, you can see a guy seemingly starting to mouth the words "Fuck you" and pulling up his hand to give me the finger.

I always enjoyed playing in the ACC because of the atmosphere. Playing hockey in Toronto is like praying in Jerusalem—it just seems special. You could feel hockey heritage when you entered that building.

Fans would often boo me, and I would cup my ear as if I couldn't hear them because they weren't loud enough. I liked to bow to Toronto fans when they would boo me after I scored a goal. One time, the stadium crew at the ACC put the Kiss Cam on me during a game and I leaned over and kissed teammate Mark Recchi on the cheek.

The 2004 goal was the last of four overtime playoff goals that I scored during my NHL career. What's interesting about those four goals is that Amonte was involved in three of them. No one on the planet knows more about how I play than Amonte does. We were playing together when we 15 years old.

In 1996, he fed me a pass that led to me beating Patrick Roy for a power-play overtime goal to beat the Colorado Avalanche 3–2 in a game in Denver. That goal ended Roy's streak of 12 consecutive overtime wins in postseason play. Considering the rivalry I enjoyed with Roy, beating him was always special. If I say that again, maybe Roy will hear me, even if he does have his Stanley Cup rings plugging his ears.

Perhaps what I should be proud about is that Joe Sakic (8), Maurice "Rocket" Richard (6), and Glenn Anderson (5) are the only three NHL players who have scored more postseason overtime goals than I did.

Those are not players who needed Lady Luck to smile upon them to find the net.

Maybe skill is more important than luck in scoring overtime goals. I can tell you there was no luck involved in scoring that goal against the Maple Leafs. That one was all skill.

FOUR

DON'T BE
CINDY BRADY

CHAPTER FOUR

Don't Be Cindy Brady

People often ask me if I ever regret the things I say when I'm analyzing NHL games on NBC. What I really regret are the numerous times I don't say exactly how I feel.

Sometimes I struggle to locate the balance between the person I really am and playing the role of a responsible television broadcaster.

Executive producer Sam Flood has joked that he would like to clamp electrodes to my nuts so he can zap me from his easy chair at home every time I ramble on too long or say something inappropriate.

It's a funny situation when you think about it. I was originally hired as an analyst because I was a colorful, opinionated person who isn't afraid to voice his opinion.

But now that I have the job the most important rule is to be careful what I say.

"Always remember to respect the peacock," Sam tells me regularly.

The multi-colored peacock was introduced as an NBC emblem in 1956 to symbolize the network's commitment to offering color programming. Today, the bird is symbolic of the network's long history of excellence. NBC is as American as hot dogs and Chevrolet.

As a traditionalist at heart, I have overflowing pride in working for this institution. To me, working for NBC is the equivalent of playing hockey for an Original Six team.

Honestly, I really don't want to do anything to dishonor the reputation of the peacock. When you are in this business, NBC is the team you want to play for. Sam is one of the best coaches I've ever known. I always listen to what he says.

I try to walk the line between being a strong analyst and being a politically correct analyst. That can be a challenging dance.

To me, it's an amusing contradiction. It's the same way in the NHL. For example, rugged defenseman Chris Pronger was celebrated for being a gritty, hard-nosed physical player who was willing to play on the outside edge of the rule book in the name of trying to win. But the minute Pronger crossed the line, the same people who lionized him for being a playoff force wanted to burn him at the stake for being a dirty player.

Should we have truly been surprised that Pronger occasionally went over the line? Teams coveted him because he was a mean, edgy player. Should NBC be surprised that I occasionally say something I shouldn't? I thought NBC wanted me *because* I was edgy.

Clearly, I'm having fun about this issue, but believe me when I tell you that Flood and I have serious discussions about it. I listen when Sam talks because I respect his experience and ability. I know he understands this business more than anyone else and he has my best interests at heart.

I'm always working to develop a happy marriage between my personality and a broadcast style that plays well to the television audience.

That struggle to develop my style has become part of my on-air personality. Sometimes I say too much, sometimes I butcher the English language, and sometimes I say exactly what needs to be said. I'm still a work in progress as a broadcaster, although I'm a much-improved performer.

Famed New York Mets manager Casey Stengel had his own language called "Stengelese," and I've also been known to make up a word or two.

One night I meant to say "abysmal" and somehow what emerged from my mouth was "adysmal."

The show's host, Liam McHugh, always does a fantastic job of making light of my screw-ups. "On this show you get good hockey analysis and a new vocabulary," he will say. "J.R. will make up new words for you. There's more to come."

I'm not afraid to make fun of myself because I always try to do the best I can with my limited education. My college education consisted of going into one class at Boston College and hearing a professor talking about a "syllabus." I didn't know what a syllabus was, and I made up my mind then and there that it was time to sign my first professional hockey contract.

"Telling it like it is and making up words is what I do best," I say when I fumble my vocabulary. "I'm not a walking dictionary."

Occasionally, I also say the wrong name. I never seem to get Dallas Stars player Antoine Roussel's name right, and I have a tendency to call Matt Duchene "Steve Duchesne" because I played many, many games against Steve Duchesne.

As soon as I make a mistake like that, my Twitter blows up with people saying I don't know the game because I got someone's name wrong. Obviously I do know the players' names, but when you are on the set, trying to organize your thoughts, with a producer chirping in your ear about how much time you have to make your point, it's easy to fan on someone's first name.

Some of the funniest moments we've had on the set of the postgame show have come as a result of some blunder that has come out of my mouth.

I know immediately when I've said something I shouldn't because I can see, out of the corner of my eye, my analyst partner Keith Jones and host Kathryn Tappen fighting to stifle laughter.

The one phrase that always causes Jonesy to laugh is when I talk about a player "coming with speed." That double entendre always makes him giggle, especially after I informed him that a woman messaged me one night on Twitter to say, "Geez, I love it when my husband comes with speed."

I'm not the only person on the show who makes mistakes, but my miscues seem to create the most humor. You aren't surprised by that, are you?

We have so much fun on the nightly show. There is a team-like atmosphere every night. It's almost like being in an NHL dressing room, preparing for an important game.

There's always a sense of excitement. Before we go live, a staff member will say, "Five minutes until we start the best show on television."

When I played for the Chicago Blackhawks, I liked to unwrap five sticks of Juicy Fruit gum before every game. I would roll the five pieces into a ball and then pop it in my mouth just before we headed out to the ice. I couldn't just shove any five pieces of gum in my mouth. They had to be Juicy Fruit, and they had to be rolled into a ball. The ball was so big that it looked as if I had tucked a wad of chewing tobacco in my mouth.

Some people would call that a superstition. Hockey players call those routines, something you do to get comfortable before a game.

Before I go on television, I like to have a coffee from Starbucks or Dunkin Donuts as I go over my notes for the night's games. It's part of my routine and helps me relax. Despite spending much of my adult life in the public eye, it's still stressful to go on television in front of millions of viewers.

In the beginning, my biggest worry was that I might pull a Cindy Brady. You remember that episode of *The Brady Bunch* where Cindy earns the opportunity to be on a television quiz show? She is all pumped up but as soon as the television light goes on, she freezes. She is like a deer in headlights and doesn't say a word. She just stares at the light and it looks like her eyeballs are going to pop out of her head.

When I first joined NBC, my concern was that the light would go on and I wouldn't have anything interesting to say. Anyone who thinks television work is easy and stress-free has never had to do it.

All of the staff members, including the camera people, help me relax because they are always energetic and full of life.

We always poke fun at former NHL player and current NBC analyst Mike Milbury, because he sometimes shows up on the set in a cranky mood. Whenever he's acting like a grumpy old bear, we let him have it in a fun kind of way. We don't like it when he brings down our mojo.

Milbury's moods are always a source of humor on the set. Mike apparently doesn't like to stay up late and he will let the expletives fly when games end up going to overtime.

When Mike starts swearing at the monitor, you know the game is tied. Mike roots for the resolution of games in a timely fashion.

His schtick is comical. He likes his role as the curmudgeon and plays it well. He has been on a healthy diet kick, and brings in fresh fruit for everyone. He's as friendly as can be, but when we go live I know he will go after me the first chance he gets.

I remember one night, after I said something that Mike actually agreed with, he said, "My God, Jeremy finally said something that is useful."

Undoubtedly, our friendly jabbing at each other makes for good television. The show is more entertaining when Mike and I disagree. Fortunately, we disagree on many nights.

Another problem that I have on the air is being long-winded. I say too much, and every time I do that Sam Flood sends me a text reminding me that he would have zapped my balls if he had the chance.

"Shorter is better and less is more in television," he always tells me.

Sam is always telling me that I don't need to throw out big words to be a quality analyst. He didn't like it when I use the word "plethora" in one of my recaps.

"Don't try to be an English professor," Sam said. "Just talk like a hockey player. Hockey players don't use the word plethora."

Of course, he is right. What works for NBC broadcaster Mike Emrick doesn't work for me. Doc has the professorial television personality, not me.

I have learned plenty from being on the set with Jones. He is the consummate pro as an analyst. I call him the "Cookie Cutter," because his analysis always comes out perfect, every time. He's predictable: he looks at the camera, looks down for a millisecond to collect his thoughts, and then he delivers an opinion that is usually right on the mark.

Jones will be critical when he needs to be, but more often than not, his analysis will be more positive than negative. I admire his focus and his ability to concentrate on what he is going to say at any given moment.

Because I look up to Jonesy, I ask him a million questions. We've become friends over time. He encourages me to write down what I want to say ahead of time. He also reminds me not to talk to the camera, that I should approach my job as if I'm carrying on a hockey conversation with the other analyst and the host.

Sam has made me a better analyst, and I've done a better job of staying out of the subject areas that cause me trouble.

That doesn't mean that I don't try to have some fun with him.

After I called San Jose Sharks forward Patrick Marleau "gutless," Sam called me out. He said it was unfair and came across as a personal attack. I understood what he was saying, and I've stricken that word from my on-air vocabulary.

But not too long after that happened, I read that a political figure called President Obama "gutless," so I couldn't resist texting Flood.

"He called Obama 'gutless'...are you going to talk to him too?" I asked.

"Don't be a wiseass, J.R.," Flood replied.

During the 2014–15 NHL season, I found myself in hot water for comments I made about Boston Bruins owner Jeremy Jacobs.

My rant was about his son Charlie, the new Boston Bruins overlord, saying the Bruins' level of play that season was unacceptable. He seemed quite perturbed by what was happening on the ice. I said I hoped Charlie remained engaged and was there to praise the team when it was performing well.

At some point, I pointed out that his dad had not been as engaged as fans wanted him to be. I said some of the Bruins players had never even met him, and that I hoped Charlie wasn't like his father.

Unquestionably, I was being critical of Jeremy Jacobs. As soon as our show was off the air, I had 10 messages on my phone. Sam wanted to talk to me immediately.

"What were you thinking?" he asked. "I was having a great night, enjoying a glass of wine, and now I have to clean up your mess."

"That was my opinion," I told him. "I grew up in Boston and that's the opinion I have of Jeremy Jacobs. I don't know the man, but..."

Sam cut me off.

"That's exactly right, Jeremy, *you don't know the man,*" he said. "You don't know his schedule. You don't know who he has or has not met on the Bruins team. You are making assumptions, and you have no facts to support that argument."

He told me that I was going to have to call and apologize to Jeremy Jacobs. As it turned out, the controversy created less of a maelstrom than he had been anticipated. Either that, or it blew over.

Perhaps Jeremy Jacobs didn't see it as a big deal or it was smoothed over behind the scenes. Either way, it was another lesson learned by yours truly: you better have hard evidence in your possession if you want to comment about a powerful person.

I was speaking more like a fan than an analyst when I talked about Jacobs. In reality, Sam was right: I had no idea how much attention Jacobs paid to his team. Just because the media doesn't see him around his team doesn't mean he isn't on the phone with his minions every day. It was an unfair comment.

As outspoken as I've been during my career, it is still not easy for me to be heavily critical of players. I do it because it's part of my job, but I don't especially enjoy ripping a player. I know what it is like to be on the receiving end of that kind of criticism.

Alex Ovechkin is the player that I've most criticized on the air, particularly during the 2013–14 season when he finished with an embarrassingly ridiculous plus-minus of minus-35. Milbury and I were frequently critical of Ovechkin's inferior all-around game. In my opinion, it was shameful to be the Washington Capitals' leader and not put a strong effort into playing a more effective style.

I'm sure Ovechkin was aware of my criticism because I've had a friendship with him for years. He pays attention to what I have to say. If he doesn't see it on television, members of his entourage will let him know what I said. Ovechkin has told me that he admired how I played when he was a young player. I wondered if my criticism would hurt our relationship.

When I was at the Olympic Games in Sochi, Russia, his entourage made it clear that he was aware of what I had said about him.

"You shouldn't criticize Alex," one said to me.

"You shouldn't be a yes man for Alex," I replied. "It doesn't help Alex if you tell him he is playing fine, even when he is not."

"He gets paid to score goals and he's scoring goals," the man said. "That's what you should be saying."

"If that is true, then you tell Alex to take the fucking 'C' off his chest," I told him. "If you are just there to score goals, then you are not a leader."

We argued back and forth, and I was keenly aware that our argument would get back to Alex.

I was prepared to lock horns with him the next time I interviewed him on the air. My first question cut right to the heart of the matter: "When you see me on television ripping you, saying you need to do things better, what do you want to say back to me?"

I paused for a second and added, "Do you want to swear at me when you hear me saying that?"

"No," he said. "If I play bad, you have to say bad things about me. It just means I have to play better the next game. If I play better the next game, you will say good things. I just have to make sure I play good, so you say good things."

"So you don't get mad?" I asked him.

"Sure, I get mad, but not at you," Ovechkin said. "I'm disappointed. I have to give you a reason to say good things."

My respect for Ovechkin grew immeasurably during that interview. He acted like a true professional. He didn't blame the messenger. He took stock of his game and concluded that he needed to perform at a higher level. I think everyone would agree that Ovechkin was a different player in 2014–15. I believe he was embarrassed by his performance in 2013–14.

When I asked Ovechkin that question, I was fully prepared for him to return fire. I wanted to give him that opportunity. I firmly believe that if you're willing to dish it out, you better be ready to get some blowback.

I think about 97 percent of the things I say about players on the air is positive in nature. I only criticize players who force me to criticize them. I can't stand lazy players or guys who display a lack of pride in what they're doing. I can't stand selfish players. Marleau and Ovechkin have made it easy for me to criticize in the past because they don't always do what's best for their teams.

That's why I have gone strong to the microphone against forward Alexander Semin. He needs to find another profession because he is shaming himself in this one. He was wasted space on Carolina's roster before the Hurricanes bought him out in the summer of 2015. It is sad that he is in the NHL because he is blocking a deserving player from coming to the show and giving a fuck about how he performs.

That may seem harsh, but can someone show me evidence that Semin was committed to helping the Hurricanes? I never saw the effort. He signed a one-year deal with the Canadiens after Carolina let him go. Good luck to them.

Sometimes I hear that players are mad about something I've said. I always hear about it third-hand, usually from people who get their kicks by stirring up trouble. Most of my so-called critics are too chickenshit to say anything to my face.

The only player who has confronted me directly is Chicago Blackhawks winger Patrick Kane. The oddity was that he was mad at me for something I said during a radio interview, even though I never actually said it.

The interview came during the 2011–12 season. The Blackhawks were in the midst of a nine-game losing streak, and, appearing on the *Waddle and Silvy Show on* ESPN 1000, I said the team needed to acquire a goalie. At the time, I didn't believe that Corey Crawford or Ray Emery was the answer. I thought the Blackhawks needed to acquire a big-name goalie, and the price would be steep. Also, keep in mind that this was happening at a time when folks in Chicago were concerned about Patrick's partying and maturity level.

"Everybody knows I am a huge Patrick Kane fan," I said. "But when you're talking something of this nature, is Patrick Kane dealable? As much as I don't want to say it, they can afford to get rid of Patrick Kane. They can afford to—with the season he's having, maybe with his off-ice reputation, maybe with the skill they have on their team. It's doable. Do I like it? No, because I love Patrick Kane. He is one of the most talented and one of the best players in the NHL. But if you really want a top-end goaltender, you're going to have to give up somebody."

Never did I say that Kane *should* be traded. I simply said there was logic to the move and that it may have made sense if they wanted to acquire a frontline goalie.

Let's also remember that Kane's numbers were down that season.

ESPN and Yahoo both picked up the quotes and they received plenty of attention, mostly because I had previously been known as a Kane supporter.

To be honest, I forgot about the whole thing until I was at the Olympics in Sochi. Kane saw me and let me have it.

"Fuck you, J.R.," he said. "You backstabbed me. You brought up my name as a guy who should be traded."

"Whoa," I said, trying to calm him down.

But it was no use. He was angry. He blew up on me and then left the building.

I didn't know how to respond. The situation really upset me. Not remembering exactly what I had said, I looked up the story on the Internet and then called him the next day. We talked for a long time. I had the interview up on my screen, and I explained exactly how the conversation started and what I had said. He told me why he was angry about it. It was a civil conversation.

Seeing Kane boil over made me feel terrible. I have always had a soft spot for him, partly because I saw some of myself in him on the ice. He is my favorite NHL player to watch. Thankfully, he said he felt better after getting the matter resolved and behind us.

Although I have been an analyst for a while, I still find myself rooting for some of my former teams. I hope for the best for the Chicago Blackhawks, the Arizona Coyotes, the Philadelphia Flyers, the Los Angeles Kings, and the San Jose Sharks. I would like to see the New York Rangers have success, because my dad owned season tickets at Madison Square Garden when I was seven. We lived in Hartford and used to come into the city for games. Having grown up in the Boston area, I also like to see the Bruins enjoy success.

That doesn't mean I'm biased for them. I can certainly criticize those teams. It's no different than being a parent. You love your child, but when he or she misbehaves, you let them know about it.

Even though I still have friends in San Jose, I have been disappointed and critical of the franchise over the past couple of seasons. There is plenty of blame to share from top to bottom, but I believe Doug Wilson has to accept responsibility. I think he's a high-grade general manager, but even quality general managers make mistakes.

After the Sharks allowed the Los Angeles Kings to rally from a 3–0 series deficit to beat them in the spring of 2014, Wilson should have had a major response. Instead, Wilson signed tough guy John Scott, who might be the most ineffective player in the National Hockey League.

How are going to improve your team if your only move is to sign a guy who historically cannot take a regular shift?

I know Wilson wanted to give his younger players an opportunity to step up, but that wasn't what his team needed. It needed a kick in the pants, a bold move, and Wilson didn't provide the lift the franchise needed.

This team needed to send a message to the players and fans that things were going to get back on course immediately. Bringing in Scott didn't tell the boys that "we expect to be better next season."

Taking the "C" off Joe Thornton was also a mistake. When the "C" was removed from Thornton's sweater, it was like stripping away a piece of the team's character. It chipped away some of the team's identity.

* * *

As an NBC analyst, I'm always in the eye of the storm. On any given night, half of our viewers agree with what I have to say and the other half see me as the spawn of Satan. That may be slightly overly dramatic, but not by much.

Fans get worked up over what I have to say about their team or their players. The radical Penguins fans have disliked me from the beginning because I played for the Philadelphia Flyers. Those two fan bases hate each other.

The rivalry between the two cities over hockey is serious and there is no end in sight. When the Penguins brought the Stanley Cup to the state capitol after winning in 2009, some of the state employees from the Philadelphia area booed when the Cup entered.

Being a former Flyer makes some Pittsburgh fans believe that I can't be objective about their players. That's just silly. I've often talked about how much I enjoy watching Evgeni Malkin play the game. In the past, I've also said that Sidney Crosby was the best player in the NHL. I don't say that anymore, but it has nothing to do with my background as an ex-Flyer.

It's not hard separating my analysis from my historical roots or personal feelings. As I said, what is difficult is leaving behind my desires to see my former teams have success.

I will admit that the Penguins have been like a burr in my side for many years. Let's not forget it was the Penguins who defeated my Blackhawks during that 1992 Stanley Cup Final. It's true that the Penguins have gotten the better of me on more than one occasion in my career.

Because of my history, there are many NHL teams that I particularly like and the Penguins are not among them. But that doesn't mean I root against them or won't treat them fairly. I will always take my job seriously and speak my mind when the cameras are on.

After all, I'm no Cindy Brady.

FIVE

GOLFING WITH GRETZKY

CHAPTER FIVE

Golfing with Gretzky

Anyone who believed that Wayne Gretzky would never speak to me again after the comments I made about him in my first book doesn't understand the nature of competitive athletes.

In my first book, I explained in graphic detail how angry I was at Wayne because of how he treated me when he was coaching the Phoenix Coyotes.

No lasting impact resulted from that passage, however, because Wayne and I understand that tension between a player and coach is as natural in the National Hockey League as slap shots and chipped teeth.

What the media and fans never realize is that it is not a catastrophe if a player and coach argue about playing time or what's happening with the team as long as respect is shown. My belief is that it is healthy for a player and coach to argue because it clears the air and allows everyone to blow off steam.

Gretzky knew how I felt about him. I respected him. Plus, I liked him as a person. He is as kind as anyone you will ever meet. But that doesn't mean I have to agree with his thinking on every subject.

Perhaps it's similar to the way some Democrats used to feel about Arizona senator John McCain. They may not always agree with all of his political stances, but most everyone in this country respects him as an American war hero.

How could you not like a man who served his country the way McCain did? It's impossible not to like McCain.

It's impossible not to like Gretzky, who always goes out of his way to do the right thing.

Even when I was mad at Gretzky as a player on his bench, I never lost sight of the fact that he is a good man. A coach-player relationship is like a marriage. You don't seek a divorce lawyer each time you disagree, or argue with, your spouse. The fact that I've been married for almost a quarter of a century is evidence of that.

Gretzky believed he was doing what was best for the team during the period when he was the coach and I was the player. I believe I could have helped that Coyotes team if he had used me the way I thought I should have been.

What Gretzky said was that he liked the way I presented our relationship in the book. He said he appreciated the kind words I said about him.

I'm confident Gretz had no issue with what I said because he and I played one of the most memorable golf matches I've ever been involved with during the 2014 playoffs. And that was a few months after the book was released.

Let me start this story by saying that the Great One's golf game has improved considerably since his daughter, Paulina, became involved with pro golfer Dustin Johnson.

We ran into each other at the Sherwood Country Club in Thousand Oaks, California, and Gretzky insisted that my twosome join his foursome. We split into two groups, and Gretz suggested that he and I play together, as well as spice up our match with a Nassau bet. That's essentially three separate bets: score on the first nine, the back nine, and for total score. It's a match play format, with each golfer awarded one point for winning a hole. No one was going to go broke with our level of wagering: we were betting hundreds of dollars, not thousands.

Because Gretzky is an eight-handicap golfer, I agreed to give him eight strokes for the entire match. I knew what kind of golfer Gretzky was.

Well, he wasn't the same golfer on this day. He was rolling in putts from all over the place

"Who are you, and what did you do to Wayne Gretzky?" I asked when he holed another long-range bomb.

By the time, he had completed the best nine-hole round I had ever seen him play, he had posted a 38 on the front side.

"What the fuck is going on?" I said. "I'm going to call Dustin Johnson and tell him to stop giving you lessons."

Gretzky couldn't stop laughing. He was having as much fun as I've ever seen him have.

Given our competitive nature, I had to "press" Gretz going into the back nine.

When you are playing for a Nassau match, a player who is two or more points down has the option of asking for a "press."

It's essentially a side bet that gives the trailing golfer a chance to even his or her money. If the trailing golfer beats his or her opponent over the remaining holes, he wins the press. A press is really just another name for a double-or-nothing bet.

The golfer leading the match can decline the request for a press, but no one does that. Gretzky wasn't going to deny me the opportunity to get even.

On the back nine, Gretzky was still playing out of his mind. I won a couple of holes, and he won a couple.

Going into the 17th hole, I was down two points and decided to press again. If I lost the press, I was going to owe him $1,500. If I won, I'd owe him next to nothing.

Sherwood's 17th is a lengthy par-3, usually playing around 228 yards. I hit it long and left, over the bunker. I was in what amounts to thick, knee-high hay. The pin was cut on the left side, giving me little green to work with.

When we arrived at the green, Gretzky started laughing because he knows the course well.

"That's death over there," Gretzky said, unable to control his amusement over the mess I've created for myself.

"Jesus, look at my lie," I said as I found my ball hidden by enough hay to make a horse's supper.

Setting up for what looked like a desperate attempt, I swung with all of my might and managed to chop the ball out of the rough, over the bunker. It stopped dead in some grassy rough between the green and the bunker.

As I walked to my ball, I saw Gretzky looking over his 10-foot par putt.

Grabbing my wedge, I took a side hill stance, plopped the ball out of the rough...and into the cup.

I proceeded to run around the green like I had just won the Stanley Cup.

Gretzky shook his head in disbelief. "That may be the best par this hole has ever seen," he said.

It may have been the best shot I've ever made on a par-3.

But Gretzky holed his putt.

"How the hell do you keep making every putt?" I asked.

"You know, J.R., I'm a pretty good putter," he said. "I have good hands."

I started laughing. "I know you have good hands," I said, "but that is a different fucking game."

All my par did was keep me even on my presses. No. 18 at Sherwood measures 444 yards, and course designer Jack Nicklaus called it the finest finishing hole he has ever created. It's a blind tee shot. Jacked up by my performance on 17, I boomed a big drive down the fairway. I followed that with a four-iron shot that curled up three feet from the hole.

I drained the birdie putt to recoup all of the money I had lost to Gretzky to that point. On that hole, I gave Gretzky a stroke. He made a bogey, which allowed me to win the press.

As I recall, Gretzky shot an 80. He should have been pleased with that score on a challenging course. Instead, he was miffed because he was sure that he was going to take me for some money until I had that miracle finish. It wasn't the money that either of us cared about. It was the competition.

Athletes play to win, especially against another athlete. I understood Gretzky's feeling of disappointment. When you are a competitor, you are always a competitor, 24/7. You don't let it go because you are competing in a different arena, or because you are retired from your sport.

One time, I won $7,500 from NBA legend Michael Jordan playing 18 holes at Butterfield Country Club in Oak Brook, Illinois. I drained a long birdie putt on 17 to close him out.

After we settled up, I started heading toward the parking lot.

"Where are you going?" Michael asked in an accusatory way.

"Heading home," I said. "Have things to do."

"Oh, no, you're not," he said. "You are going to give me a chance to win my money back."

"We don't have time to play another round of golf," I insisted.

"No, we don't," he said. "That's why we are going to the gin room."

No one says "no" to Michael Jordan. I threw my clubs in the car and followed Jordan to play cards.

Two hours later, I left without the $7,500 I had won on the course, plus $1,000 of my own money. I was livid because I had allowed myself to be sucked into that trap. Jordan is a quality gin player. He destroyed me.

"You set me up," I said to him as I paid up. "I know that because I thought I was setting you up."

I could relate to the disappointment Gretzky felt at Sherwood Country Club. It was a win that got away from him.

That was probably the best two-hole finish I ever had on a golf course. I didn't win anything. All I really did was tie Wayne Gretzky in a round of golf. But it felt like I had won the U.S. Open.

Gretzky would have never let me live it down had he beat me at Sherwood.

That's why he wasn't angry over what I had said in my book. He understands how competitive both of us are. I admitted that sometimes I acted like a petulant child when I didn't get the ice time I wanted, but I still believe Gretzky made a mistake in how he used me. But as a former player, Gretzky understood those feelings.

All he said about the book was that he appreciated my honesty.

* * *

The only real complaint I heard about my first book was regarding my decision not to reveal the identity of my former teammate who boasted a penis the size of a "baby's arm."

Every player who played with him knew exactly who I was writing about, because once you lay eyes on his Louisville Slugger in the dressing room, you don't forget it.

I don't remember any other mammoth penises I've ever seen in the locker room. But I remember that one.

The truth is I had many discussions behind the scenes about whether I should name him in the manuscript. A female lawyer and I had a frank discussion about that passage. The argument centered on whether a male would be embarrassed or proud to be known for swinging an extra-large bat. I can honestly say that I never once anticipated that my life would include having a 30-minute discussion about the size of another man's penis with a woman I didn't know.

When the discussion dragged on for more than my attention span would allow, I brought it to an end by announcing that I would call the player and ask him if he cared whether I announced to the world that he is one of the most generously endowed men on planet earth.

As it turned out, he did care.

Much to my surprise, my former teammate elected to keep his penis size private. He works for a company outside of the sport of hockey, and he didn't want the size of his manhood to become the subject of chit-chat around the water cooler.

That was all I needed to hear. This player is a first-class man and he was a first-rate teammate. If he didn't want his dick to be known as the eighth wonder of the world, I had his back. There is no statute of limitation on being a good teammate.

Undoubtedly, it's difficult to top a story about a giant penis. But I have recalled a couple of tales from my playing days that offer similar shock value. One involves the punking of teammates, and the other story centers on the consequences of a teammate's skirt chasing. (Warning: an animal was harmed in the making of the second story. Animal rights advocates, pet owners, and cat lovers are not going to enjoy this tale.)

Let me start by saying that current NHL players seem less inclined to participate in risky behavior than players in my era. The AIDS epidemic, fear of sexually transmitted diseases, and the reality that social media can turn your private affairs into public spectacles in seconds has altered players' behavior.

But when I was playing, the single guys liked to think of themselves as playboys. Skirt chasing was a frequent topic of conversation in the dressing room, and coaches would warn players that sex wears you out. Coaches would have preferred that players take a vow of celibacy during the playoffs.

"It saps your leg strength," coaches would say.

But players know the truth is that it's not the sex that takes your legs—it's staying out until 3:00 in the morning chasing the sex that saps your leg strength.

It was commonplace in my day for guys to tell stories about their sexual conquests, and this is one story I've never forgotten. I'm not going to say what team I was playing for when it happened, or even the city where the incident occurred, out of fear of providing enough information for someone to identify the player.

This is what could be called the "pussy story" for a couple of reasons.

The story, as they always seem to do, starts at a bar where a teammate meets a beautiful young woman in her midtwenties who invites him back to her high-rise apartment. According to my teammate, they were in the living room making out when the woman excused herself to slip into the appropriate attire for what was about to occur.

Now alone in the room, my teammate was hanging out on the sofa when a previously unseen cat strolled over, hopped onto the couch, and started doing what cats do: rubbing against my teammate.

It should be noted here that my teammate hates cats with unbridled passion. He repeatedly pushed the cat away with force, irritated that the feline was violating his personal space. Eventually, it was the cat who became angry, and he dug a claw into my buddy. It turned out to be a fatal decision by the cat. Remember, this guy had been in a bar most of the night. In an instant, he grabbed the pussycat, took a few steps to a sliding door, opened it, and tossed the cat over the balcony railing.

The kicker here is that the woman lived on the 35th floor.

When the woman returned, she took no notice of the cat's absence. She had other thoughts on her mind. They retired to the bedroom. There was no mention of any cat, although attention was paid to a pussy. When the joint mission was completed, my teammate climbed out of bed, dressed, left the apartment, and never saw that woman again. She never tried contacting my teammate to see if he could offer any insight into her missing cat. Maybe she believed the cat escaped somehow. When she discovered it missing, it probably didn't occur to her to think that the guy she banged the night before had murdered her cat. Maybe she thought the cat escaped when my teammate left the apartment. Maybe she thought my teammate stole the cat.

In telling the story the next day, my teammate insisted after he had exited the apartment that he went searching for the crime scene. It wasn't ghoulish curiosity. "I wanted to see if he really did land on his feet," he told us. He said he never discovered the body.

My pranking story begins at Caesars Palace during one of the San Jose Sharks' preseason trips to Las Vegas. The players always organized one trip before the season started, and another after the playoff run was finished.

Teammates Torrey Mitchell, Devin Setoguchi, and I were sitting at a table playing blackjack when a fellow player engaged us in conversation. It all seemed like normal chit-chat, as we complained and celebrated about how the cards fell. He was a friendly guy, and after several hands, it felt as if we knew this guy. At one point, he told us about a party he had been invited to attend. He said it was an exclusive event, invitation only. He said he couldn't attend but that we should go. He said it was destined to be the most memorable and wildest party we'd ever seen.

He jotted down the address for us. "The password is Dakota," he said. "They will not let you in if you don't know the password."

Mitchell, now with the Montreal Canadiens, and Setoguchi, now playing in the American League, both liked the idea of heading out to this party for a while to see what it was all about. The party was off the Strip, out in the Las Vegas suburbs. We hired a limousine, and when we arrived at our destination, we found ourselves on the front steps of a beautiful, ornate mansion.

We rang the doorbell and a gentleman wearing a tuxedo answered the door.

"Yes?" he asked.

"We are here for the party," I said.

He didn't move.

"Dakota," Mitchell said, and suddenly the door opened wider and we were ushered inside.

It was like a scene from the movie *Eyes Wide Shut*, starring Tom Cruise and Nicole Kidman. It was a large, open room with 30 to 40 partygoers milling about. The lighting was odd and the music playing was odder. The ambience had an eerie, surreal feel to it, about two shades below creepy.

Mitchell was feeling bad vibes almost immediately.

"This is weird," he said. "We may not be here all that long."

A blond, almost white-haired man, who bore a resemblance to the assistant coach character Dauber on the 1990s TV show *Coach*, walked over to us and started asking whether we belonged at this party.

"This is invitation only, select company, you understand," he said with meaning. "Who invited you?"

"A man sat at a casino table and told us about it," Mitchell said.

"What's the password?" he asked.

"It's Dakota," we all said in unison.

Passing muster didn't quell Mitchell's fears. "We need to get the fuck out of here," he said. "Right now. I don't like this."

About this time, a beautiful woman entered the room wearing only a pair of skimpy panties. She was escorted around the room by a well-dressed man who encouraged the patrons to touch and feel her as she made the rounds.

When he stopped to see us, he said simply, "This is who you will be having tonight."

Beautiful naked woman or not, Mitchell still wasn't having it. Setoguchi didn't say much. I learned later that he wasn't pleased to be there, either. But playing my role, I told everyone to relax. I just wanted to see what would happen next.

On cue, the lights were lowered, a door opened, and everyone in the room slipped on demonic masks. Mitchell froze, but in his mind he was halfway out the door.

Next, a hospital gurney was wheeled in. A sheet covered an object on the table. "It's a fucking body," Mitchell said.

Within moments, the sheet was removed to reveal the same beautiful woman we had met earlier...with her chest and torso sliced open. All of her organs were exposed. The masked-partygoers gathered quickly around the table, sorting through her body parts. A man picked up her liver and took a bite. "Tastes like chicken," he said.

I don't know whether Mitchell heard those words or not, because he was already on the move. I began to hightail it to the door as if my life was in peril. After a few steps, I was intercepted by what appeared to be a guard. Mitchell and Setoguchi saw the man stab me with a large knife. Blood appeared to be gushing from my body.

What Mitchell and Setoguchi didn't know was that when we arrived at the mansion, I had gone to the bathroom and been fitted with a blood pouch by a special effects expert.

The whole scenario was devised by the Syfy channel's *Scare Tactics* hidden-camera comedy/horror television show. The show's premise is simply to use special effects and make-up artists to create cliché horror film scenes and scare people in real life. The show launched in 2003, and it's still on the air today.

Producers find people who are willing to set up friends or family members—or in my case, my teammates—for the amusement and entertainment of a television audience. I had called show executives and convinced them to build a show around NHL players. I volunteered to turn some of my San Jose Sharks teammates into show victims. They loved the idea.

Stunt workers and special effects experts on this show are top of the line. Everyone in the house that night was a professional actor. The woman lying on that gurney looked as if she had been expertly cut open by a medical examiner. It could not have looked more realistic.

To aid the realism, I had paid the man at the blackjack table $200 to tell us about the party. I thought it would seem more realistic, and make Setoguchi and Mitchel more intrigued, if it seemed as if we were crashing an exclusive event. When that guy told us about the party, it seemed like we were receiving a hot tip on a horse before a big race.

It was my hired hand who came up with the password idea.

Each *Scare Tactics* episode is supposed to end with someone coming out and asking the victims if they are scared, and then announcing, "You shouldn't be, because you are on *Scare Tactics*."

But Mitchell couldn't be told that because he was probably several miles away from the mansion when he stopped running. After seeing me gutted in a knife attack, Mitchell had climbed atop an L-shaped bar to survey the room for exits. He first attempted to knock out a 16-foot picture window. When he did not succeed in that attempt, he leapt off the bar and raced toward another window. He tore through the metal blinds and jumped through double-pane glass. Bleeding and terrified, Mitchell looked like an Olympic sprinter as he raced headlong into the night. He wouldn't answer his cell phone, even when he saw it was my number. Maybe he thought someone was using my cell phone to pinpoint his location.

Setoguchi didn't go anywhere, saying later he was too petrified to run. Shocked by what he had just witnessed, he had embraced the warped idea that people in mansion wouldn't kill and eat him if he acted as if this was all normal.

Once Setoguchi was let in on the joke, we called Mitchell continuously for 30 minutes before he answered his cell phone and was told that the entire event was staged as part of a television show. He suffered only minor injuries, including one to his pride after being fooled like that. He probably should have gone to the hospital to receive a couple of stitches, but he wrapped up the cuts and soldiered on. Once he recovered from the shock, he thought the night was hilarious.

I had successfully scared the hell out Setoguchi and Mitchell. Unfortunately, the night didn't turn out to be a success for the *Scare Tactics* producers. They had rented a private home to film this, and Mitchell had caused damage with his great escape. In addition to crashing through a window, he had destroyed the claws on a bearskin rug as he raced across a floor.

Plus, the San Jose Sharks organization flexed its muscle and made sure the Mitchell-Setoguchi episode never aired. San Jose team officials didn't believe players should be portrayed in what they considered a "negative light."

Obviously, I was disappointed by that decision. Show producers did give me a copy of the video from that night. It is great. That night was only supposed to be step one of our plan—I was going to bring out San Jose stars Joe Thornton and Dan Boyle on the next night. Wouldn't that have been fun?

In hindsight, it was probably a blessing that I didn't end up getting Boyle involved. After seeing how that episode evolved, I would have worried that, given Danny's personality, he might have suffered a heart attack when the sheet was pulled off that woman.

SIX

LEMIEUX VS. GRETZKY

CHAPTER SIX

Lemieux vs. Gretzky

When I started playing in the National Hockey League in 1988–89, the debate was about who was the third-best player in the league. It was a given that Wayne Gretzky and Mario Lemieux were the best two.

In some hockey fantasy leagues, Gretzky was considered two players. You could draft either his assist total or his goal total. Having both was considered unfair.

From the time I was 10 until I was 17, Gretzky was the only Hart Trophy winner the NHL knew. He won the award eight consecutive seasons from 1980 through 1987. Essentially, Gretzky was the NHL's best player throughout the Ronald Reagan presidency.

Lemieux won the Hart in 1988, and then Gretzky won again in 1989. In their heyday, they were like Zeus and Poseidon competing against mere mortals.

In my first NHL season, Lemieux totaled 199 points and Gretzky came in at 168. That's two seasons' worth of points for today's elite players.

Gretzky and Lemieux both averaged better than two points per game that season. In 2014–15, the NHL only had three players who averaged *one* point per game.

When my Chicago Blackhawks lost the Stanley Cup Final against the Pittsburgh Penguins in 1992, Lemieux, who needed an equipment man to lace his skates because of his back problems, won the Conn Smythe Trophy after scoring 16 goals and finishing with 34 points in just 15 games.

If Lemieux hadn't played for Pittsburgh in that series, could we have defeated the Penguins? Impossible to say, because they were a quality team. But here's what I know for sure: the Blackhawks were an exceptional team that season and the Penguins were far less dangerous without Lemieux.

In May of 2014, famed national radio host Dan Patrick forced me on a live show to answer the question about which of the players I would rather face. That's like asking if you would rather be struck by a bus or an 18-wheeler.

I resisted at first but he pestered me enough that I felt I owed him an opinion. I didn't want to answer out of respect for their greatness. Plus, they were distinctively different kinds of players. Gretzky was a slick thinker who darted in and out of traffic to find time and space. Lemieux was a large, bullish man with incredible hands and a powerful skating stride.

Honestly, can anyone truly say which player was more dangerous?

It's not an answer that you are providing. You are merely stating an opinion.

Since I'm not known for being wishy-washy, I decided to say Gretzky was better.

"You're a suck-up," Patrick said, laughing.

I reminded Patrick that I was at odds with Gretz when I played for him in Phoenix. Sometimes in interview situations, the safest answer is not to play the game. But I'm a player, and player's play. So I gave Patrick my opinion.

If I would have said Lemieux was better, he would have had another smart-ass answer.

Most of the players in the league were in awe of Gretzky and Lemieux. They were playing a far more advanced game than the rest of us were. It was like we were playing checkers and they were playing three-dimensional chess. It was commonplace for fans and players alike to open their newspapers and go directly to the scoring summaries to see how many points Gretzky and Lemieux had the night before.

For hockey fans in the 1980s and 1990s, the excitement of watching Gretzky and Lemieux was probably similar to what baseball fans experienced in the 1920s and 1930s when they watched Babe Ruth play on the diamond.

Most fans, I believe, miss the days when we were blessed with players who could produce unforgettable performances on a regular basis.

The truth is that in this era, there is no consensus on who the best player in the league is. Some would argue that Sidney Crosby is the best but I don't believe he is. He allows himself to be pushed out of the big games too much. You can make the argument that Crosby has never really had the right complimentary wingers. However, I don't accept that argument. I counter that Lemieux and Gretzky showed they were the best, no matter who they played with.

To be sure, the game is different now. In my day, the primary objective was to score goals. Today, the primary objective is to prevent goals.

Crosby is an exceptional player. But in my judgment, to be the best player in the NHL, a player should be dominant in the postseason and capable of lifting his team to a higher performance level. I don't see that from Crosby.

Since winning a Stanley Cup in 2009, Crosby's Penguins have lost three Game 7s and been swept once in the playoffs. As of this writing, Crosby has three goals in his past 18 playoff games. That's a pace for a 15-goal season. He hasn't come close to matching the heroics of his former landlord, Super Mario.

Sorry, Pittsburgh fans, but Crosby doesn't even make my top five players. Neither does Washington's Alex Ovechkin.

If I were named director of hockey operations for an NHL team and could have any player in the NHL, my first choice would be Jonathan Toews. I believe he is the best player in the game today.

To give you an idea of how I evaluate talent, here is my list of the top players in the game after the 2014–15 season, regardless of position:

Jonathan Toews (Chicago Blackhawks)

In baseball, scouts like to find five-tool players. Toews is a seven-tool hockey player. He can score, create plays, defend, win faceoffs, play gritty, kill penalties, and lead.

He's clearly the best captain in the NHL today, and certainly he will rank among the greatest captains in NHL history. Already, you can put him in the conversation with Bobby Hull, Stan Mikita, Denis Savard, Glenn Hall, and Tony Esposito for the unofficial title of Greatest Blackhawk.

Obviously, Toews will need to log a few years in Chicago to cement his place, but leading the franchise to three Stanley Cup titles puts him in the aforementioned company. Plus, he's not close to being through. There is more greatness to come from Toews. He clearly hasn't had his best season yet.

Drew Doughty (Los Angeles Kings)

Even after watching Duncan Keith dominate the 2015 playoffs, I still believe Doughty is the game's best all-around defenseman. In my opinion, that was proven when both Doughty and Keith played for Canada at the Olympics. No offense to Keith, but Doughty is the lead dog on that sled.

Like Keith, Doughty can play 30-plus minutes per game. Doughty is a three-zone defenseman, capable of making important plays everywhere on the ice.

In the playoffs, we've all seen that he has some magic with the puck on his stick. If he wasn't playing for Darryl Sutter, Doughty's offensive numbers would be much more impressive.

Patrick Kane (Chicago Blackhawks)

Statistics can be both telling and misleading, but in Kane's case they explain why I have him listed as the league's third-best player.

The Blackhawks won Stanley Cup championships in 2010, 2013, and 2015, and in those three playoff runs Kane totaled 30 goals.

Kane has 114 playoff points in 116 career postseason games. When the games are meaningful, he finds the spotlight. This is a clutch player. He is a dangerous, scary, highly competitive offensive force.

Kane is only 27, and he's already probably on the list of the top 20 American-born players of all time. He has three Stanley Cups, an Olympic silver medal, and 557 points in his first 576 games. Enough said.

Carey Price (Montreal Canadiens)

Unless you are the quarterback of the Dallas Cowboys or Green Bay Packers, I don't know of an athlete who faces more scrutiny than the goaltender for the Montreal Canadiens.

The Canadiens goalie is always being compared to Montreal's long list of goaltending heroes such as Jacques Plante, Ken Dryden, and Patrick Roy.

Price deserves his place on my list because he has earned his way into that illustrious group. In 2014–15, Price was the best player in the game, period.

The Hart Trophy goes to the player who was deemed most valuable to his team. No one was more valuable to his team than Price was to the Canadiens.

Without Price, the Canadiens might not have even made the playoffs. His goaltending carried that team. He seems to have the perfect temperament to handle the Montreal pressure.

Henrik Lundqvist (New York Rangers)

The New York Rangers won 39 playoff games between 2012 and 2015, and Lundqvist is the main reason for that level of success.

The Rangers are scheduled to pay him $10 million in 2015–16 and he is worth that money. His $8.5 million cap hit is money well spent. He is a big-game player. Whenever the Rangers have an important game, Lundqvist steps up. Since 2012, he has won more than 75 percent of his playoff elimination games.

His consistency separates him from other goalies. The New York players have incredible confidence that Lundqvist will make the saves he needs to make.

Lundqvist might also be the best-dressed man in the NHL. He would fit as well as a model for *GQ* as he does in an NHL sweater.

John Tavares (New York Islanders)

Tavares is one of the smartest players in the game and a guy who is capable of carrying his team.

Much was made about how the arrival of Johnny Boychuk and Nick Leddy solidified the Islanders in 2014–15, but Tavares is, by far, the primary reason why this team is successful.

Regardless of whom he plays with or what is happening on his team, Tavares finds a way to make an impact on the game. He is not as flashy as some of the top players in the game and yet there he was competing for a scoring title at the end of the 2014–15 season. His efficiency is off the charts.

Duncan Keith (Chicago Blackhawks)

During the 2015 playoffs, teammates and commentators began to run out of ways to praise Keith. Marian Hossa called him "unstoppable." Coach Joel Quenneville called him a "freak" because he can log so many minutes. At one point during the Stanley Cup Final, a reporter asked Quenneville whether Keith might be able to play an entire game, without rest.

Obviously, that wouldn't be in the best interest of Keith or the team, but it would be fun to see what level he would be at in the third period. Sometimes, it sure looks as if he could play 35 to 37 minutes and still be effective.

After the Blackhawks had dispatched the Lightning, Keith was the unanimous selection for the Smythe Trophy.

What separates Keith from other defensemen is that he is equally effective as a defender as he is as an offensive contributor. In a one-on-one defensive situation, is there anyone you would want out there more than Keith?

Steven Stamkos (Tampa Bay Lightning)

Stamkos is a 40-goal scorer who can also help his team without scoring.

He might be evolving the way Tampa Bay general manager Steve Yzerman did when he was a player with the Detroit Red Wings. Yzerman was an offensive force when I first entered the NHL, but as his career progressed he began to be a more complete player.

In my opinion, Stamkos is more physical than Yzerman was. He will throw a heavy check. He's meaner than Yzerman was. If Stamkos can be as physical as he was in the 2015 playoffs and still be a 40-goal scorer, he could be a $10 million player if he tests the free agent marketplace in 2016. The consensus is that he will stay in Tampa Bay and continue his quest to win a Stanley Cup.

Sidney Crosby (Pittsburgh Penguins)

It's been well established here and elsewhere that I've always wanted more from Crosby, especially since he has come back from his concussion issue. But coming into the start of the 2014–15 season, I still considered him the best player in the game. My opinion on that has changed.

I've wanted him to be the kind of player who will carry a team the way Toews or Tavares can. We haven't seen that from Crosby in a long period of time.

I want him to be a Mark Messier–type of captain, the kind of guy who says we are going to win tonight, instead of telling the media that we hope we will play our game or we hope we control the game.

All that being said, Crosby is certainly a top player. If he hadn't missed so many games this past season, he probably would have won another scoring championship.

Alex Ovechkin (Washington Capitals)

In his first season under coach Barry Trotz, Ovechkin took a step toward becoming a more complete player.

He's still not quite there yet, but it is clear to me that he is making an effort to change his ways. If he becomes even an average defensive forward, he would have to be in the top three players in the game because he is the most proven and dangerous goal-scorer in hockey.

The man has six 50-goal seasons in an era when every coach is designing his defensive scheme specifically to prevent Ovechkin and other stars from scoring.

Ovechkin receives plenty of criticism, much of it deserved. But I will defend him as one of the most important players in the game today. I don't see anyone else in this league with his scoring credentials.

Here are the two guys on the bubble for my top-10 list:

Victor Hedman (Tampa Bay Lightning)

If you evaluate Hedman as an athlete, you might convince yourself that he could have been a shooting guard on Sweden's national basketball team if he had gone down a different path.

He is an elite athlete, a 6-foot-6 defenseman who skates as if he's 6-foot. I don't know if I've seen a player his size skate with the same drive he has.

Hedman proved during the 2015 playoffs that he is an elite defenseman, probably a 2016 Norris Trophy candidate. If the Lightning had won the Stanley Cup, Hedman might have won the Conn Smythe Trophy. He was the Lightning's most important player. He's on the verge of cracking my top 10.

Ryan Getzlaf (Anaheim Ducks)

I'm always left wondering why Getzlaf is not a 30-goal scorer. But that doesn't change the reality that he has an incredible impact on every game he plays.

Every team in the Western Conference thinks about its depth at center based on the knowledge that it has to match up with Getzlaf, a big man who handles the puck with the flair of a smaller center. Getzlaf can hold his own against any center in the NHL.

* * *

A team has to have stars in order to win in the NHL. But it's the undervalued top players who make a difference in the playoffs.

If I ever get in a position to run an NHL team, I will be looking for the players whose effectiveness may be flying just under the radar. Here are 10 more players who are underappreciated but could play on my team any time:

Joe Pavelski (San Jose Sharks)

Over the 2013–14 and 2014–15 seasons, Pavelski scored 78 goals. That makes him one of the top goal-scorers in the NHL over that period. He's been a proven 30-goal scorer for four seasons, but somehow he doesn't get the notoriety he deserves with the national fan base.

The general impression of Pavelski is that he's a good player; the reality is he is an elite player.

Anton Stralman (Tampa Bay Lightning)

He might be the most underrated player in the NHL today. He's a top-pairing defenseman who can be a shutdown guy and still contribute to the team's offensive attack.

He has taken on more responsibility in Tampa Bay. Coach Jon Cooper said it best when he said that Stralman will never win the Norris Trophy, but he can help his partner win it. His partner is Victor Hedman.

Jaden Schwartz (St. Louis Blues)

Schwartz is a classic hockey player, a forward who is above average in every aspect of the game.

Consistency is his trademark. Schwartz's coach knows what he is going to get from him every time he puts him in the lineup. He never cheats on his effort. He plays each game as though the entire world is watching him.

Alex Killorn (Tampa Bay Lightning)

Be honest—did you pay any attention to Killorn before the 2015 playoffs?

The Nova Scotia native played at Harvard, and he has developed into a strong top-line winger. He does the little things well, and puts himself in position to score big goals.

To me, he looks like he could be a consistent 25-goal scorer.

Mats Zuccarello (New York Rangers)

You realize Zuccarello's importance the most when he's out of the lineup.

He's a smart, quality player who will do whatever it takes to be successful. He's an example of a smaller player whose size isn't a factor. Size is still important in the NHL, but it isn't the roadblock for players that it once was.

Brent Seabrook (Chicago Blackhawks)

If the Blackhawks are in overtime, Seabrook is a good bet to score the game-winner.

The man has a history of rising up in big games, and yet we rarely see him listed among the top defensemen in the NHL. Well, I'm saying it here.

Andrew Ladd (Winnipeg Jets)

Ladd has been one of the most underrated players in the NHL for years. Because he has bounced around a bit in his career, it's easy to forget that he was a significant contributor to the Blackhawks' 2010 Stanley Cup championship.

He has offensive touch and some bite to his game. You win with players like Andrew Ladd. If I was managing an NHL team, I would be looking for players who have Ladd's characteristics.

Marian Hossa (Chicago Blackhawks)

Some might argue that Hossa is too popular to be on this list, but I still don't believe he receives enough credit for the depth of his ability.

People view him as a goal-scorer whose best seasons are behind him, but I see him as a two-way forward, the type of player coaches love during the playoffs. He's a second-line winger who can score goals and keep the opposing team from finding your net. He's also a very dependable player along the boards.

Kyle Okposo (New York Islanders)

Okposo has quietly developed into the power forward that every team is looking for to round out its roster.

He's big, rugged, and I wouldn't be shocked if he ends up scoring 40 goals one season.

Mike Fisher (Nashville Predators)

Fisher is a two-time lottery winner. First, he is a handsome, rich, well-respected NHL player. Second, he got to marry one of the world's hottest singers in Carrie Underwood.

This sounds ridiculous to say, but I believe Fisher has been a better player since he got married.

My theory is that his life is so good that he goes to the rink every day unburdened by all of the things that can get in the way of success. Because Nashville is Music City, Fisher is playing in a city that is perfect for his career and his wife's career. They just had their first child.

It's all good for Mike Fisher. What I see now is a player who is one of the best No. 2 centers in the game today.

Honorable Mention: Wayne Simmonds (Philadelphia Flyers)

When I analyze games, I see many players who come up with big performances every couple of weeks. What I notice about Simmonds is that he makes a play or two that gives his team a chance to win each and every night.

Simmonds is one of the best net-front presences in the NHL today. He spends so much time in the low slot area in front of the goalie that he should be paying rent.

* * *

If you look closely at the lists I've provided here, I believe you can get a good sense of how I view the game. I played the game with heart, and if I managed a team, I would want it known as a team that plays the same way.

SEVEN

JUST SIGN HERE

CHAPTER SEVEN

Just Sign Here

It's impossible for an athlete to escape stardom these days. In a world connected by the Internet and social media, there is nowhere to hide. Once, I was at the top of the Eiffel Tower in Paris and someone recognized me.

Even though I've traveled extensively around the globe, I've never found a place where I was anonymous. Someone always knows my face.

That's a problem for some athletes, but it has never been a problem for me.

You can choose to be annoyed by your celebrity status, or you can choose to revel in it. From the very beginning of my NIIL career, I've accepted the reality that interaction with the fans is a job requirement of an athlete or a TV celebrity, as I am now.

It's enjoyable to me because I like to make people happy, and it doesn't require much effort on my part.

I understand that some of my teammates through the years didn't share my enthusiasm for talking to fans. I understand that signing autographs can be inconvenient at times. Athletes are no different than anyone else. We have places to be, people to see, and schedules to keep. When we are done with our workday, we want to go home like a normal person.

But I've always felt that the rewards that come from talking with fans far outweighed the schedule disruption it caused me.

One time during my career, I was eating with teammates when someone came up and asked one of the guys for an autograph.

"Do I know you?" my teammate asked the fan.

"No," the man replied, confused by the question.

"Good, then let's keep it that way," he said, waving him away like he was dismissing a servant.

I won't name the player because he is a good man who was probably having a bad day. But when I've seen that happen, it occurs to me that it required more energy to reject that autograph request than would have been expended if he had scribbled his name on a piece of paper for the guy.

If he would have provided that guy with an autograph, he would have had a fan for life. Instead, the man sulked away and probably concluded that the player he previously admired was an asshole.

Unless I'm totally pressed for time, I will sign anything you put in front of me. There are people in every NHL city who stand outside the rink, and they will ask you to sign multiple items. Many of the items I sign end up for sale on eBay or at collectibles shows.

When I was playing, some of my teammates said I shouldn't do that because the autograph seekers were profiting off my time and signature.

But here's my position: I don't care if other people make money off my celebrity status. In fact, I'm glad some people have received a financial benefit from my career. Good for them. They are involved in a legal enterprise. It's not as if they are stealing my signature. They put in the time. They travel to the rink and wait for me to come out. Most of them are polite. Who knows what these people would be doing if they weren't peddling autographs?

Plus, let's be real here. I've made more than $70 million in salary and endorsements during my NHL career, and I still make a steady stream of income from my celebrity status. I am still paid handsomely to make appearances.

How much more could I have earned if I had charged for my autograph? An extra $100,000 or $200,000? I would rather be a good person and make fans happy than fret about an extra $100,000 in income. I've signed as many as 40 hockey cards at one time for a person.

Some of these dealers tell me I'm one of the best signers in the game, and I'm proud to have that reputation.

When I'm away from home, my fan mail and autograph requests pile up at my house. Fans have admitted that they have paid a fee online to find my home address, just to send me items to sign.

Tracy organizes it all for me. When I get home from the road, Tracy has placed every hockey card in the self-addressed stamped envelope that the senders have provided. She makes sure that I don't fall too far behind. I receive an incredible number of baseballs to sign. Not sure why a collector would want a hockey player to sign a baseball, but I do it. One Chicago Blackhawks fan even mailed me his high school diploma to sign.

The only time I'm reluctant to sign is when I'm pressed for time or when I'm sitting in a crowd at a hockey game. If I sign one autograph during a game, there will be a line within seconds. There will be one person there, then quickly three or four, then a half-dozen. After several minutes of signing, I will have a line stretching up the stairs. If that happens during a game, dozens of people are inconvenienced because their vision of the game is blocked by my autograph line.

If fans ask me for an autograph during a game, I always tell them to meet me at the top of the stairs after the period.

I've certainly had moments when fans become too pushy or verbally abusive or rude. That happened to me one night when I was playing on the road in Vancouver.

When players come into an arena, there can be 100 people waiting there, hoping to get an autograph. You don't have time to sign for everyone but I always tried to sign a few. On this night, I signed three or four and then started to head into the arena.

I stopped right in my tracks when a guy called me an asshole for bypassing him. "Typical athlete," he said. "Too good to stop and sign."

He picked the wrong night to insult the wrong person. I turned around and got into his face. "You are a typical autograph seeker," I said. "You don't have any appreciation for anyone except yourself. Do you think I have time to sign for everyone here? I did what I could."

The man was so stunned by my response that he actually took a step backward. He could tell that he had struck a nerve and he was clearly apprehensive, maybe even fearful, about what I might do next.

"And just to show you what a fucking good guy I am, give me your puck, because I'm going to sign it."

He reluctantly pushed the puck toward me and I signed it. "You're welcome," I said. "Would a typical athlete have come back and signed that puck?"

I'm confident the man didn't envision having that exchange with me.

The next time I was in Vancouver the same guy was there waiting for me. He apologized for what had happened the previous visit.

I often put my number beside the signature. I usually write 27, but I will write 97 if I know it's a Philadelphia Flyers fan. I put effort into it, just like the players from the Original Six era did. There is a major difference between how today's athletes sign compared to how the stars of yesteryear did. If you've ever seen an item autographed by Gordie Howe, you will notice that he has perfect penmanship to go along with his perfect collection of hockey talents. Montreal great Jean Beliveau's signature was as graceful as his game. Chicago Blackhawks legend Bobby Hull has a distinct autograph with flair to it. I believe my autograph has some flair to it, like Hull's.

Occasionally, I will have people come up to me and say, "Can you give me a good autograph?"

"What do you mean?" I ask. "I always put a distinct signature on the item."

"Too many guys scribble," people say. "I want to be able to read the name."

To be honest, I can provide you with an autograph that makes it possible for you to read every letter. But that's not my signature. If you showed that signature to an authority on NHL autographs, he would tell you it was a forgery. There are two sides to a request for a legible autograph: you might end up with something that has my name on it but you haven't really received my true signature. When you sign autographs, consistency is the key. I've signed the same way for years, and people know what my signature looks like. You can't read every letter, but you can tell it's my name.

I'm sympathetic to the fans who like to collect quality autographs. A lot of modern athletes do scribble illegibly. Blackhawks star Marian Hossa and NHL legend Mario Lemieux have two of the worst autographs I've ever seen, and they are among two of my favorite players.

The dedication and passion that autograph collectors have borders on amazing. When I was at the 2015 Stanley Cup Final, I flew into Tampa at 11:30 PM the night before Game 5. I stepped on an elevator and the doors were closing when a hand reached in to stop my forward progress. Four guys stepped in with a plate full of pucks for me to sign.

I started laughing.

"Don't any of you have lives?" I asked. "It's almost midnight on a Friday night. Don't you guys have someone at home prettier than me to meet?"

This kind of scenario happens to me regularly. If I'm making an appearance in some city, I always find someone waiting for me at my arrival terminal with pucks and cards to sign. They know my flight number and arrival time. The only possible explanation is that they have moles at the airport who tip them off when celebrities are taking trips. There is no other possible explanation.

I've signed more than every conceivable kind of hockey item— I've also signed my name on women's breasts, hips, and other body parts. Most of the breast-signing was done in Canada. Those fans are crazy in a fun way.

Back when I was playing, a young mother asked me to sign her baby's forehead one day in Chicago. The kid was probably seven or eight months old. I felt as if I was guilty of child abuse. I almost said "no" to this one. I wondered whether it was possible for a baby to be poisoned by the ink.

"Are you sure you want me to sign this baby's noggin?" I asked.

"Yes," she said. "I'm going to wash it off, but I want to take a picture of it first."

Several times I've been asked to sign the hoods of sports cars. One guy had me sign his white Porsche 911.

"Make it big," he said.

I whipped out a Sharpie and created a three-foot Roenick signature covering his hood.

One night, I was at Stanley's Kitchen and Tap in Chicago and a young woman came up to me and asked for an autograph. As I pulled out a Sharpie, she asked me to list the "craziest" places I had placed my signature. I gave her the rundown.

"Have you ever signed a woman's vaginal area before?" she said.

"No, that's a new one," I said.

"Good, then I can be the first," she said. "Will you do it?"

"Okay," I said.

She hiked up her skirt and pushed aside her panties ever so slightly. It was not as awkward as it sounds because she was careful to make sure I didn't see anything that mattered. I had enough skin to write on and not enough to make a determination about whether she was sporting a playoff beard or not.

That had to be strangest autograph request I've ever received. Do you think she did that to show her boyfriend?

* * *

One of the rewards of being an athlete is the opportunity to meet fascinating people. I've met legendary athletes, people of incredible wealth, famous politicians, world leaders, and inspirational human beings.

Jack Jablonski falls into the latter category. On December 30, 2011, Jablonski was playing junior varsity high school hockey for Benilde–St. Margaret's in Minnesota when he suffered a spinal cord injury that left him a quadriplegic. He had scored a goal in the first period. In the second period, he was pursuing a puck toward the boards and was being chased by two players from Wayzata High School. The first player hit him in the back and the second player pushed him toward the boards. His face slammed into the boards. People knew instantly that Jablonski was severely injured.

He had been one of my Twitter followers, and after we heard about his situation, Tracy and I decided to go see him. What I discovered is that he is one of the most inspirational people I've ever met. He didn't let that tragedy end his life. He is now a student at the University of Southern California. He's a great kid. He has become like a son to me.

That doesn't mean he won't try to put me in my place. When I'm on the air for NBC and say something he doesn't like, my phone blows up with text messages from him.

One night I mentioned that Minnesota Wild forward Thomas Vanek wasn't pulling his weight. The Wild had signed him to score goals, and he simply wasn't scoring enough.

"Lay off my buddy Vanek," Jack texted. "He will come back and show you."

I appreciate that Jack has a special bond with the Wild, because many of those players have been highly supportive of Jack since he was severely injured. Vanek, in particular, has been a friend to Jack.

"Jack," I texted, "it's not my job to protect your boys."

I told him he should be texting Vanek and telling him to rediscover where the net was located.

"He is making it easy for me to criticize him," I wrote.

"Understood," Jack wrote. "But lay off him, anyway."

Jack is never shy about telling me what to say on television. Even though he is keenly aware that it's my job to critique player performances, he constantly tells me to lay off his Wild players because criticism was putting too much pressure on them.

No one can poke fun at me the way Jack can.

When the Wild lost 12 of 14 during one stretch of the 2014–15 season, I suggested it was probably time for the Wild to fire Mike Yeo. As the words were coming out of my mouth, I was thinking, *I will hear from Jack about this one.*

"It's not the coach's fault," Jack texted me. "You have to tell the Wild to go out and trade for a goalie. Their goalies aren't any good."

That was right before Minnesota general manager Chuck Fletcher traded for Devan Dubnyk.

Jack knows the game. I believe he has a future in the management side of the game if that's where his interests continue to lie.

Considering that a tragic occurrence during a hockey game robbed him of a normal life, it would be cool if the hockey world gave him an opportunity to work in this business.

Jablonski has an amazing attitude, especially given the struggles he has endured. If I ever think for a moment that I've had a bad day, I try to remember what Jack has gone through and how he carries on with his life.

You never know who you will meet in this business. In my last book, I told the story of Darcy Walsh, who I met when he asked for my autograph when he was still a boy. Now he is one of my closest friends.

It's impossible to be involved with all of the incredible people you meet in the business, but you should try to do what you can. I get paid to speak, and one of the jobs I enjoy most is when I'm asked to speak at a school.

When I speak to students, one of my primary themes is the importance of having all-encompassing respect. I tell them they need to have respect for themselves, their classmates, their teachers, and for the work they are doing.

I want them to take pride in what they accomplish each day and I encourage them to make honor part of their lives.

"If you see someone cheating in class," I ask them, "would you tell on them? Or would you tell them not to cheat anymore? Or would you ignore what you witnessed?"

That's a very difficult question for young people to answer, because peer pressure is a staple of student life.

Plus, many youngsters don't have respect for themselves. If they don't respect themselves, how can we expect them to respect a friend enough to tell him or her that it is dishonorable to cheat during a test?

One of my messages is to care less about what other people think about you and instead be proud of who you are.

To accomplish that, I start dancing on stage without any music. For the next 60 seconds, I bust out every move I can think of to embarrass myself in front of several hundred students.

Usually, the auditorium is filled with laughter, and then I stop and ask, "How many of you thought I looked like an idiot up here?"

In most cases, everyone raises their hands.

Then I ask, "How many of you dislike me now because I was different than you expected me to be up here?"

Nobody raises their hand.

"I think we learned something here today," I say. "I think we learned that we won't necessarily be disliked if we are different. So don't be afraid to be different, to take chances. I just embarrassed myself up here and it didn't hurt a bit. In fact, I enjoyed it. And if someone doesn't like me for being different, that's their problem. I don't lose sleep over what people think of me."

My point is obviously to convince kids that they shouldn't live their lives giving in to peer pressure.

The right answer to my question about cheating is to be a friend first and try to convince the cheater not to. But if the person doesn't respond to your effort, then it is important to tell someone in authority. I try to convince students that turning in a cheater is not ratting him or her out. You may be helping someone who doesn't know he or she needs help.

My belief is that by causing a cheater minor trouble, you are probably sparing him or her from more serious problems down the road. The cheater will get in a small amount of trouble from a teacher, but that is nothing compared to the amount of trouble a cheater might get in if he continues that unethical behavior as an adult. Sometimes you have to look at the bigger picture.

When I speak in front of corporate groups, I usually alternate between giving motivational messages and simply telling stories about my life as a NHL player.

I often talk about Mike Keenan teaching me that fear can be both your ally and your enemy at the same time. Fear of failure can overwhelm you; it can smother your drive and ambition. If all you think about is failing, you will likely fail.

Keenan taught me to use fear as fuel. I never thought about the act of failing itself, just the consequences of failure. I thought about how Keenan might bench me, or trade me, or kill my career. I always played my best hockey in the NHL when I was worried about what Keenan might do to me. If I wasn't a NHL player, who was I? That question terrified me. That Keenan might have enough influence to get me pushed out of the game frightened me so much that I never gave him anything except my best effort. I wasn't going to let Keenan take hockey away from me. You dig deep when you think like that. You push yourself to be the best you can be. That attitude will serve you well in whatever career you have. The idea that you must protect what is yours has probably been around since the dawn of man. If you want to keep what you have, then you have to make sacrifices.

In whatever career you choose, there will always be a boss who is looking to intimidate you or someone who wants your job or someone who wants to prevent you from achieving what you want to achieve.

That's a fear you should embrace. Let that fear become your driving force.

Sometimes, companies have paid me simply to show up and hobknob with guests and staff members or to sign autographs.

One time, Frito-Lay hired me to come to its national meeting. I was with a stable of big-time athletes. I remember former Notre Dame and NFL quarterback Joe Theismann was there, along with ex-Dallas Cowboys Tony Dorsett and Daryl "Moose" Johnston.

We were paid to attend the company's showcase party and sign autographs for two hours. At the two-hour mark, the athletes all filed out like they were hourly employees, punching out, at shift change.

I stayed for the party. I figure if you pay me to come to a party, I ought to show you a good time.

At one point, I went up and sang a couple of songs with the band. I did my go-to karaoke rendition of "Funky Cold Medina," plus the disco song "Boogie Nights."

I believe that if I'm being paid to attend your event, I should give you my best. I want the people paying for my services to believe they got their money's worth. My objective is to make sure that no one who shows up at the event leaves disappointed.

I have a good reputation in this world for going above and beyond what is asked for me.

That's why I've earned good money in this world since I stopped playing.

After my first book was published, I made an appearance at a Barnes and Noble bookstore. The schedule said I would be there from 6:00 to 8:00 PM. Barnes and Noble closes at 11:00 PM and at that point I still had a line stretching out the door.

The manager let his employees go home but stayed to coordinate the signing process. We didn't leave until 1:00 AM. We sold hundreds upon hundreds of books that night.

I feel like if people are going to take time out of their day to come and see me, I can spend a few extra minutes to make it worth their effort.

That's the philosophy that guides me during promotional appearances. Frankly, that's how all athletes should view these situations.

Usually, whoever is paying the bills makes it worth your time to be there. Multiple times I've been paid to show up at golf tournaments and once even to be a guest at a bar mitzvah. You show up, you schmooze, you sign autographs, and you try to make people happy. I'm pretty good at giving people their money's worth, if I do say so myself.

Once, in Phoenix, a woman paid me to show up to play pick-up hockey with her husband. He and his buddies were getting ready to play and suddenly I showed up and announced that I was there to play on her husband's line. I set him up for a bunch of goals and we celebrated every goal like we were playing in an NHL game. It was a blast. His wife had purchased plenty of beer and set it up to look like I had brought it.

We sat in the dressing room, drank beer, and did what men do after beer-league games. People have told me that I act as if I'm having a good time at my promotional appearances. The truth is that I *am* having a good time. I enjoy being around people. I feel fortunate to be able to make a living by simply being who I really am.

It doesn't always go perfectly when you make an appearance. I made multiple promotional appearances for Coors Beer, and most of them were at bars and restaurants. Those events drew overflowing crowds. But then organizers decided to send me to a grocery store, located 40 minutes outside of Chicago, and it was far less successful.

Sitting at a table located between the produce section and the alcohol aisle, I was surrounded by more bananas and Brussel sprouts than fans. In fact, there were no fans at all when I showed up.

Finally, a youngish long-haired guy, dressed like a factory worker, walked in and marched directly to the beer cooler, where he yanked out a case of Bud Light. When he turned around, he spotted me at the table and his jaw dropped.

"Whoa, dude," he said. "What are you doing here?"

"Coors Beer brought me in to sign autographs," I said.

"Whoa," he said. "I didn't think I would ever meet you, and certainly not in a grocery store."

He explained to me that he had stopped to buy some Bud Light before the next Chicago Bears game.

"But I'm here representing Coors," I reminded him.

"Then, bro, I'm buying Coors," he said, marching back to the cooler.

He had me sign his case of beer, one of the only autographs I signed at that event. I'm sure Coors appreciated that I converted a Bud Light drinker, if only for one day.

EIGHT

CHIP AND A
PUTT OFF THE
OLD BLOCK

CHAPTER EIGHT

Chip and a Putt Off the Old Block

The first time my son, Brett, served as my caddy for the 2014 Lake Tahoe Celebrity Golf Tournament, I ended up with my best finish ever. That wasn't a coincidence.

By my estimation, Brett's advice saved me several strokes over the course of a three-day, 54-hole tournament. I ended up tied with retired LPGA star Annika Sorenstam for second place, finishing seven points behind former NFL quarterback Mark Rypien under the Stableford scoring system.

At 17, Brett is more advanced as a golfer than I was at his age. He is more technically sound. His swing is prettier. When I was 17, I was a grind-it-out golfer.

Brett has a golfer's mentality. His game is structured and more under control than my game was in the late 1980s. His game is calmer. He is more conservative in his approach, which is amazing given his age. When I was a teenager, I needed to scramble to earn pars and birdies. I could score in the 77-79 range for 18 holes, but I didn't look as smooth as Jordan Spieth when I was doing it. My day at the course was often a wild-ass roller coaster ride.

When I was a teenager, all of my good rounds were stress-filled. My son can shoot 77 or 78 and make it look like a walk in the park.

Brett aspires to play college golf, and I don't see why he wouldn't be able to do that. He hasn't lost a match in high school. His best score is around par.

At Lake Tahoe, we argued several times about shots, and every time I listened to him it turned out to be the correct decision. He reads greens amazingly well. I probably made four or five putts I would have misread if he had not been with me.

Usually, I'm a hard-ass when it comes to trusting my own golf instincts. I'm a quality player and I'm confident in my game. But I knew it was time to trust my son.

The best example of my trust in him came on the No. 13 par-4 hole when my ball was buried in a bunker. I had a downhill lie. I planned to open up my club face with the hope of getting underneath the ball and scooping it onto the green.

"Dad," Brett said. "You need to close your club face and hit down on the ball. If you open it up and get under it, the ball won't pop up. You have to dig down. Close your club face and loosen your hands. Let the club hit sand and then open up as it goes down and wedges the ball up."

His explanation made sense to me. I executed as instructed and the ball popped onto the green. The ball stopped four feet from the hole and I drained the putt.

Once on a par-5, my drive didn't carry well down the fairway. I was still about 230 yards short of the green when I pondered my second shot. Instinctually, I pulled out a three wood, ready to muscle up with the idea of still reaching the green in two.

My son took away the wood and offered me a seven iron.

"We can get there," I said.

"Maybe, but the traps here can hurt you," Brett insisted. "The trap on the right has a big lip, and if you push into that lip you have no chance for a birdie. If you hit to the left of the green, it's a tough up and down from there."

I listened to what he said, and took the seven from him.

"Go with the odds," Brett continued. "If you hit that seven, then we go right into your best club, which is the 60-degree wedge."

Just as Brett predicted, I hit the seven and left myself about 100 yards. I plopped a wedge in tight, and knocked it home for the birdie.

The 2014 Celebrity Tournament at Lake Tahoe was the first time I played there without ever coming close to losing my temper. Brett's presence forced me to play a calmer, safer game, but I didn't lose any of my competitive juices. It became an enjoyable tournament, made more fun by the fact that we were contending for a championship on the last day.

The funny thing is that being competitive in that tournament was a secondary consideration. My main objective was to make sure that Brett had a fun and memorable experience. I owed it to him because I am a father who is proud of his son.

Brett told Tracy before the tournament that he was worried either I wouldn't listen to him or I that would become angry if his advice didn't work out. Hearing that made me feel like an asshole. Any father who cares about his child never wants him or her to be afraid to talk to him. I was determined to make sure I was on my best behavior.

To be honest, I understood that Brett had something to offer to my game. My son is 6-foot and 180 pounds but he can out-drive me by 50 yards. Although my golf game has improved through the years, his swing is much more professional-looking than mine. And he has a good eye for the course. He understands how a course should be played.

He thinks his way around the course, and I will my way around a course.

When I'm in my competitive mode, I can lose my mind momentarily. The Phil Mickelson–designed Whisper Rock is a prestigious course in Scottsdale, Arizona. The folks who manage that course demand the game be played properly. Those good people didn't believe I was playing properly several years ago when I damaged a golf cart windshield after I wrapped my driver around a tree.

Playing the fifth hole, I snapped the ball out of bounds. Then my mind snapped. As the driver struck the tree, the head flew off and smashed into the windshield. To say club officials weren't happy with me would be an understatement.

I've played many angry rounds of golf in my life. In fact, I recorded my third hole-in-one 10 years ago on No. 17 at Whisper Rock when I was completely pissed off.

I was angry because on the par-four No. 16, I had recorded a bogey after I chose to use an eight instead of a nine-iron. I couldn't let go of my mistake. I was still bitching as I stepped into the No. 17 tee box. The guys in my group, including my former Phoenix Coyotes teammate Ed Jovanovski and my friend Mike Young, quickly grew weary of my moaning.

I was again trying to decide which club to use.

"Quit complaining. Take your nine-iron and knock the ball in the hole," Young said.

"Okay," I said, and struck the ball.

Right when I made contact, Young said, "I'll have a scotch on the rocks," meaning that would be his drink order when we celebrated the hole-in-one.

The ball flew directly into the cup. No bounce. No roll. In the cup, on the fly. You could hear a thud when it struck the bottom of the cup. I was celebrating, and when I turned around to look at Young, he gave me one of those friendly "you're an asshole" looks. All of that bitching I did and then I record an ace. Hardly seems fair, does it?

But those stories, plus the stories I told earlier about my behavior at the Lake Tahoe event, help explain why having Brett on my bag was a wise decision. With Brett as my co-pilot, I would be on my best behavior, and his knowledge would give me a fresh approach on the golf course.

The Lake Tahoe event is a highly competitive tournament. Mark Rypien is my kryptonite. I simply can't beat him. Actor Jack Wagner is also a highly competitive golfer, a threat to win every year. He is remembered most for his role as Frisco Jones on the soap opera *General Hospital*. Wagner's attitude on the golf course reminds me of Brett Hull. Hullie and Wagner play like they don't give a fuck about anything that is happening there or elsewhere. It must help them keep their emotions from getting in the way of their games.

These are not two guys who are worrying about what's happening in the Middle East when they're at the tee. They play a relaxed style and that serves them well.

Once at Donald Trump's Wonderful World of Golf, the defining moment came when we were walking up the fairway with Donald and he was marveling at Hull's game. Hull does have a pro-style

golf swing but I pointed out that I had the advantage on the hole
we were playing because I had gone flag hunting and stuck my shot
three feet from the pin. Hullie was going to be looking over a tricky
40-footer.

"I have him on this hole," I told Trump.

"We will see about that," Hull said.

When we reached the green, Hull quickly looked over his putt,
made his read, and then struck the ball. As soon as he made contact,
he said, "There it is," and started walking toward the hole.

The ball dropped right into the center of the cup as if it had been
drawn there by a magnet. Trump went nuts. "He called that shot!"
Trump said.

Rattled by the turn of events, I missed my three-footer. Hull shot
a 67 that day, and I shot a 72.

"He's an asshole but I love him," I said on the broadcast.

The athlete who surprised me the most on the golf course
was NBA Most Valuable Player Stephen Curry of the Golden State
Warriors. He is as skillful on the golf course as he is at draining
three-pointers. His chipping is unbelievable. His iron play is
fantastic. He is a slick putter. I was shocked. Given how gifted he
is on the court, when did he have time to develop a golf game like
that?

The field at Lake Tahoe improves every year. In 2014, former
LPGA champion Sorenstam joined the field. Just one more reason
why it was probably the perfect time to join forces with my son.

I am quite serious about my golf game. Since moving from
Arizona to the San Diego area, I have put a green in my backyard
with hitting areas located at 55, 85, and 125 yards.

The entire Lake Tahoe experience humbled me in ways that are hard to describe. The natural father-son relationship involves the dad as the teacher and the son as the student. But at some point the relationship begins to evolve, especially when it is time for the dad to admit that he could benefit from the son's help. That's where we were on this weekend.

When you are a pro athlete who travels regularly, you always worry about whether you are being a good parent. My son plays hockey and I made sure that I was never overly involved, because when I look back at my own childhood I recall that my parents were too involved. Once when I backed down from a confrontation, I heard someone call me a "pussy." When I looked into the stands, I realized it was my mother.

My father was too hard on me. He once made me walk home three miles in the dead of winter because he didn't like the effort I put in during a hockey game. I didn't have a childhood as much as I had a hockey road trip.

We never celebrated a traditional Thanksgiving because I was always going to a hockey tournament. We would eat a turkey dinner on Wednesday. Even at Christmas, we would eat early and then hurry out the door to head to another tournament. Everything in the Roenick household was scheduled around my hockey career, for better or worse.

When I was 13 and living in Virginia, it cost my parents $25,000 for me to play with the New Jersey Rockets. Because it was a 250-mile trip, they would put me on a People's Express flight from Dulles Airport to Newark every Friday.

On some weekend road trips, we would drive through the night, and I wouldn't arrive home until an hour or two before dawn. A couple hours later, we would start the entire process all over again.

Was that insane behavior? Or was it loving behavior, because my parents understood that I had gifts that would allow me to be a star in my sport? Those are challenging questions to answer.

I respect my parents for pushing me to be the best I could be, but I also resented them for not allowing me to be a kid sometimes.

It's clear in hindsight that I rebelled against my upbringing by carousing more than I should have when I first entered the NHL. Always sheltered by my parents, I wasn't ready to handle the responsibility of being an adult. Clearly, I was also angry at them for being tough on me. Even though I loved hockey, I wanted more non-hockey normalcy than they allowed me to have. It took me a while to figure that out.

When I became a parent, I vowed that I would never allow myself to be a hockey dad. I didn't push Brett into hockey. I didn't go on the ice and try to turn him into a mini-me. Whatever he was going to achieve in hockey, he was going to do it without my hands-on-attention. Golf has been the sport where we have bonded.

I'm so proud of the man my son is growing up to be. When this book is published, he will be a senior at Westminster Prep School in Connecticut.

Brett grew up in Arizona, where he attended public school. But Tracy and I wanted him to go to prep school back east, the same way we did. We believed that it would give him the best opportunity to get into a good college.

He looked at several schools. I remember we looked at Avon Old Farms, where Brian Leetch became a hockey star.

"It reminds me of Hogwarts from the Harry Potter movies," Brett said. "I'm not going to school at Hogwarts."

He decided to apply to only two schools, Westminster and Kent, and he felt fortunate to be accepted into both.

He got into these schools partly because he interviews well. He always comes across as a genuinely warm person. It comes through that he cares about other people. He shakes your hand when he meets you, and 15 minutes after you meet my son, you may get a text from him, saying he enjoyed meeting you.

This is a kid who dresses in a coat and tie when he serves as commissioner of a fantasy draft.

He decided to attend Westminster. It hasn't been easy for him. He went from Arizona public schools where he never had homework to a school that essentially treats students as if they are already in college. As a freshman, he had homework every night and had to learn how to study for the first time.

The easy road would have been to move to a less challenging school. But Brett would not quit. He has battled his ass off and has made himself into a B student.

After his sophomore year, his golf coach in California suggested that perhaps Brett should move back home and play golf at a local school. I know Brett would love to make a career out of golf, and if you want to be a pro at any athletic endeavor, you have to put your heart and soul into it. You have to live that dream 24 hours per day, seven days a week.

I believed he would jump at the chance but that's not what happened. Brett didn't even ponder the decision for 15 seconds.

"I don't want to do that," he said. "Westminster is the school I want to graduate from. If I can get through Westminster, I can go to any college I want."

He was adamant for another reason.

"Twelve hundred kids applied to go here, and how many did they take? Was it 100?" he said. "They took me because I was a good kid. If I leave now, it would be a kick in the face to the 1,100 who wanted to go here and couldn't because I got in."

His determination and the mature, adult way he looked at that decision made me tear up. I had never been prouder of my son than I was at that moment. He has grown into a fine young man. I don't have to parent Brett. I just have to be supportive of the choices he is making.

As much help as Brett provided me in the Lake Tahoe tournament, I still couldn't win. But because Brett was with me, even making a run at the title seemed like a success instead of a failure. Usually, I leave the course feeling as if I lost the tournament. That didn't happen in 2014. I left the course feeling as if Rypien simply won the tournament with his strong play. He wasn't going to be beat that day. His 33 points in the final round tied the tournament record set by former NFL quarterback Billy Joe Tolliver in 2010.

I think Brett helped me play as well as I could have played. What I see now is that Brett is developing that competitive edge an athlete needs to truly be the best. I think that's the final piece to his game. You can't just hope to win. You have to want to win more than your opponent. You also have to expect to win. I've had that desire since I was a kid.

When we were competing together at Lake Tahoe, I could see that competitiveness growing in my son as we worked to stay in contention. While he was helping me get the most out of my golf game, maybe I was helping him discover his competitive fire.

The day before I wrote this chapter, Brett and I were on the course together and he fired a round of two over par. I was one under. My son has never beat me yet in a round of golf, and the quest to do that fuels him. It's making him a better golfer. He is getting closer and closer. I've noticed that he shows some controlled anger now when he doesn't make the shot he expects to make. Tracy and I have been waiting for that competitive side to show itself.

Obviously, both of his parents are highly competitive people. His mother is competing at a high level in dressage and I've been an NHL player. We haven't pushed him, but maybe we have shown him by example.

Today, he's a teenager who wants to be the best he can be at whatever he does. He was proud when he started to out-drive me on the golf course and I was proud for him, because I remember the pride I had when I started to drive a golf ball farther down the course than my father.

My only advantage over Brett now is creativity and experience. I know where to put the ball and where not to put the ball, and I have more knowledge about how to grind out a good score. Brett is a thinker, but he is too young to know what he doesn't know about golf. He will understand the game better as he grows older.

I can stay in the moment better than he can. I can string together several good holes because I focus on one hole at a time. He thinks ahead too much because he's still only 17. He has lapses in concentration that I don't have.

As a parent, seeing my son excel on the golf course makes me feel like I've done something right. Maybe by helping him sort out his golf game, I'm actually helping him sort out his life. Anyone who has ever played sports knows that the lessons you learn competing serve you well in everyday life.

Because of my hockey and television careers, I didn't have the same relationship with my children as other parents do. I simply wasn't home as much as other fathers. That is something that always worries me.

As I previously mentioned, I didn't go on the ice with Brett because I was concerned I would transform into my father. Brett loved hockey but he never gravitated to it the way I did at his age. I never felt any need or desire to yell at him about his hockey playing.

Here is a story that I will never forget. When he was eight or nine, Brett came up to me and asked, "Can you break your back playing hockey?"

"Of course, you can," I said. "It can be a very serious injury."

Since then, he has played game the more cautiously. He has always been a thinker, and even at a young age he reached the conclusion that the rewards of hockey didn't outweigh the risks.

I thought about that conversation when I heard the story about Jack Jablonski's injuries. I'm thankful that my son was never injured severely playing hockey. I'm thankful that he followed me into golf and not hockey. By the way, Jack and Brett have become friends.

Throughout my NHL career, I gave plenty of thought to what I should be doing to help my children grow up to be well-adjusted human beings. The real challenge of parenting is that there rarely is a right or wrong answer. Sometimes, the answer is A. Sometimes it is B. Sometimes it's all of the above or none of the above. It all depends upon your child's personality. What's right for your son might not be right for your other son or daughter. Sometimes you believe you are inspiring your child when he or she feels you are being overbearing. And sometimes you don't say anything when you should be trying to inspire your child to spread his or her wings.

It's the most complicated job in the world, and it's made more complicated by the fact that you love your kids to death. Here's the unspoken reality about parenting: you will eventually figure out how to do it well, but by then your children will be adults and probably have kids of their own. That's why almost everyone is a good grandparent.

I'm not there yet. I'm still trying to inspire my children to be the best they can be. I hope both of them understand that I'm doing the best I can.

To add more fuel to Brett's golfing fire, I've told him that I will give him $1,000 if he can beat me in three consecutive rounds before he reaches the age of 20.

My hunch is that he's going to collect that $1,000. Maybe I'm a better parent than I think I am.

NINE

THE COMMISH

CHAPTER NINE

The Commish

When you are asked to talk to NHL commissioner Gary Bettman, it is like being summoned to the principal's office.

He has a commanding presence, an air of authority. Unquestionably, he prefers hockey matters to be handled the way he wants them handled. He doesn't appreciate when underlings go off the script. He always makes that abundantly clear.

In 2013, I was involved with a group of businessmen looking to put together a bid for an expansion franchise in Seattle. My name kept appearing in media reports and I knew Bettman wouldn't like that. He likes the work behind the scenes to remain behind the scenes.

When I was in Toronto to attend my buddy Chris Chelios' induction into the Hockey Hall of Fame, Bettman cornered me for a chat.

It wasn't a principal-like lecture that I received. It was more like he was offering fatherly advice.

"Jeremy, I see your name mentioned often in media reports about putting a team in Seattle," Bettman said. "We talked about this, didn't we? We need to do everything in the proper order. I think we are getting a little ahead of ourselves. Don't you agree?"

It was the politest way anyone has ever told me to shut the fuck up.

The truth is that I admire Bettman and I believe he has done a quality job as the NHL commissioner.

Of all the shocking declarations that have spewed out of my mouth through the years, that is the one that stuns people the most. It certainly stuns Chelios, who has a long history of being at odds with Bettman.

Chelios isn't alone in his anti-Bettman sentiment. The commissioner is booed almost everywhere he goes, and the majority of fans seem to believe he has hurt the game.

But I think we should be giving Bettman credit for guiding the NHL out of the dark ages. Doesn't anyone remember what a low profile the NHL had in the United States before Bettman became commissioner?

You hear people say that Bettman ruined the game with expansion, but I think the game is in fantastic shape right now. There is a reason why multiple North American cities are seeking an NHL expansion franchise.

League revenues were at $400 million when Bettman was hired in 1993 and now they are approaching $4 billion. It won't be long until they are at $5 billion. Players should genuinely thank Bettman when they see him because every time he grows the game, they benefit.

People bitch about the NHL expansion into the Sun Belt, but the Florida expansion franchises were already in place when Bettman was chosen to be the league's commissioner. He put expansion teams in Nashville and Columbus, and those seem to be working out fine.

All the Predators and Blue Jackets need to officially cement their long-term place in the hockey world is a Stanley Cup championship.

I would argue Nashville is one of the more popular road destinations for NHL players and fans. A night in Tootsie's is enough to appreciate NHL expansion to the south.

Plus, whether players accept it or not, the NHL has a much better business model with the salary cap in place. Competitive balance is a reality. The gap between the top NHL teams and the teams just missing the playoffs is only a few wins in the standings. Franchises are more stable.

I understand why fans blame Bettman for the 2004–05 lockout and the canceled season, but that fight was inevitable. Bettman works for the owners. There was never any doubt about that. It wasn't a surprise. And whether players admit it or not, most of the players knew we were eventually going to end up giving in on the salary cap.

Does anyone believe players' lives have been dramatically harmed by the introduction of the cap? I don't think so.

Probably, it has had a negative impact on some of the stars. Without a cap, we would surely have more players earning more than $10 million per season. But it seems the tradeoff is we have more players earning $5 million. The NHLPA would prefer a free market, but you can make an argument that the salary cap has made it easier to grow the game. Players and owners both benefit from growth.

My appreciation of Bettman's strengths as a CEO-style leader grew as I talked to him about the potential for a franchise in Seattle.

It's clear me that Seattle is the most attractive destination for an NHL expansion team.

The city would help solve the NHL's need for two more teams in the Western Conference. The team would be close to Canada and a natural rival for the Vancouver Canucks. Seattle is a vibrant market with a hockey history. It's the 14th-largest American television market. The only missing pieces are a new arena suited for hockey and a strong ownership group.

The investment team I joined hoped to fill that second piece. What I wanted was to head up the hockey operations side of the business.

After I set up a meeting with Bettman, I prepared my boys for what to expect. I told them that Bettman is cordial and good humored, but he is also protective of his turf and very direct when it comes to the issues of his league. He likes well-organized plans, not general concepts and fuzzy ideas.

"Don't let him intimidate or fool you," I told my group. "He knows exactly why we are coming in, and he knows exactly what we've been up to. But he will make small talk and then he will say, 'So, gentleman, what can I do for you today?'"

Sure enough, we show up in his office and Bettman summons in his cabinet, including deputy commissioner Bill Daly. We talked for a couple of minutes before Bettman sat behind his desk, folded his hands, and said, "So, gentlemen, what can I do for you today?"

All of the guys in my group were chuckling or stifling laughter. I laughed aloud because I had nailed my prediction of how Bettman would greet us.

Obviously, I learned a lot from talking to Bettman that day. I'm glad I went through the process, even though it became clear after a while that this wasn't the right time or deal for us. Entrepreneur Chris Hanson was leading the charge to get a new arena and that effort centered on landing an NBA team.

Even though it didn't work out for me, I still believe the NHL has to end up in Seattle. I believe Las Vegas will work, too.

But I can tell you that Bettman will only put teams there if he is satisfied that all of the requirements for long-term success are in place. If you want to join Bettman's club of owners, you have to survive his scrutiny.

I feel that Bettman treats me with respect. In fact, he always goes the extra mile to be friendly. If I'm at Nick and Stef's Steakhouse in Manhattan before a New York Rangers game and he is there, he will always come over to say hello and introduce himself to my guests. He is a very gracious man.

Now, this doesn't mean I've agreed with everything Bettman has said or done. When I was playing for the Philadelphia Flyers in 2004, the NHL suspended me one game for throwing a water bottle in the direction of referee Blaine Angus. I had become incensed over his non-call against Buffalo Sabres defenseman Rory Fitzpatrick for knocking out a tooth and cutting me with a high stick. I lost more than $91,000 in pay.

Bettman went on Toronto radio and agreed that Angus should have called Fitzpatrick for high sticking, but then implied that I had been fortunate that the NHL only suspended me one game instead of three games.

That sent me off on my second tirade in two days.

"He forgot that the NHL merged with the WWF and we hide razor blades in our pockets and cut ourselves so we can get calls," I told the media after Thursday's practice at the Flyers Skate Zone. "Somebody better remind him we did that. I'm just surprised that you can get fined $91,000 for throwing a water bottle on the ice. It's like fining Gary Bettman $91,000 for throwing all those lies about the bargaining agreement coming up. He throws those around like they're candy. The NHLPA should fine him for those."

I was referring to the ongoing negotiations between Bettman and NHLPA executive director Bob Goodenow, during which Bettman cited how many teams were losing money. A month after the Angus incident, in February of 2004, I accidently started a debate with Bettman over the growing tension during All-Star weekend in St. Paul, Minnesota.

I was carrying the union flag that weekend, saying players were ready to play in Europe or would start their own league if the owners locked us out.

"We've got our roots dug in just as much as owners do," I told the *New York Times*. "I don't think somebody like myself or Keith Tkachuk or Mike Modano—we don't need to play another game in the league if we don't have to. A lockout is not good for the game. If the owners want to say it's going to take two or three years, I'm wondering how many years I'm going to play anyway."

At the time, I believed it was ridiculous that both sides seemed committed to carrying on this fight to the point of canceling the season if necessary.

"I think it's [scarier] for the sport and for the owners than it is for the players," I said. "The players can go play in Europe. They can play in different leagues. But the owners are going to lose their franchises, and they will have to deal with people who work for them; they will have to deal with the building that will sit empty. The Buffalos, the Carolinas, are they going to stick around? Is Ottawa going to stick around? Calgary? Edmonton? Those teams are not going to be able to withstand one or two years. There's going to be a lot at stake, there's no question."

That *New York Times* article included a sentence that reads, "Bettman said the situation was not nearly as dire as Roenick portrayed It."

When I look back at some of the things that escaped from my mouth, I can only conclude that Bettman must have viewed me as an annoying pain the ass. He has never said that to me, but it has to be true.

It seemed to be a running joke in the hockey world that I wasn't Bettman's favorite player.

On July 26, 2005, a satirical website called TheBrushback.com published a fictional story about Bettman's changes to the following season. It reported that starting in 2005–06, the red line would be eliminated, goalie pad size would be reduced, and "it will be illegal for Jeremy Roenick to talk." The website even fabricated an explanation from Bettman. He was quoted as saying the rule was implemented "out of sheer desperation."

"We respect the fact that he speaks his mind and isn't afraid to ruffle feathers," the made-up Bettman quote continued. "Unfortunately, he just can't seem to get his point across without pissing off our entire fan base. Therefore, if Jeremy Roenick opens his mouth in public, he will be fined. If he does it a second time, his teammates will be fined. A third offense and we're going after his family."

At the end of the satirical piece, they made up a quote from me launching verbal missiles at the NHL for placing the fictional gag order on me. I blasted the league with a profanity-laced speech at the same time I was insisting that I would abide by the rule.

Now that is some funny shit.

Obviously, the story was written after I went on my now-famous tirade at the Mario Lemieux charity golf tournament in the summer of 2005. That's the one where I said that people who believe athletes are spoiled can "kiss my ass."

That event was covered in my first book, and there's a video of it on YouTube. It was not my best day on the planet. I'm sure that's the primary reason why TheBrushback.com penned the satire. You have to have a sense of humor about these things.

If you review the history of what I had to say about relations between the owners and the players, you can see that my perspective changed over time. I was a devout union man during the 1994 lockout, and was still spouting the party line heading into the 2004 lockout.

But as the lockout progressed and I looked at the situation, I became convinced that the introduction of a salary cap wouldn't permanently damage the players. Given the amount of money we were earning, it seemed shortsighted to fight this battle on principal. In my opinion, with or without a salary cap, NHL players were always going to be richly rewarded.

As a general rule, players don't know much about the business of hockey. Players only think about playing. When I was a player, I was naïve about the hockey business. I believe that is true for most players. I would bet if you asked Boston Bruins president Cam Neely, or Los Angeles Kings president Luc Robitaille, or Pittsburgh Penguins owner Mario Lemieux, or Tampa Bay Lightning general manager Steve Yzerman, they could make the same statement. When you are a player, you believe that you are the product, the drawing card, and owners are raking in millions off your ability.

The truth is that the NHL, even with a salary cap and growing revenue, is still a business that requires considerable effort to be profitable. I believe Bettman has done an impressive job making the NHL a quality business venture. When you look at how franchise values have risen over the past decade, you realize he has done good work setting up the league for the future.

Parity has helped keep ticket sales strong. The competitive balance is impressive. Not much needs to be done, although I believe there is room for improvement.

The NHL needs an NFL-style replay challenge system to correct huge mistakes before it is too late. While I was writing this book, the competition committee, made up of team executives and players, agreed to approve a coach's challenge for the purpose of reviewing video of a goal to see whether goaltender interference or other infraction should change the call. But that's not enough. We need to have an all-purpose coach's challenge that would give coaches the opportunity to challenge any call, or lack thereof, that they believe is critical to the outcome of the game.

Because the NHL is now a $4 billion business, this is becoming even more important. Bad calls undermine the integrity of the game and they could potentially cost a team millions of dollars.

Let's look at the 2015 playoffs series between the Washington Capitals and the New York Rangers. With the Rangers leading 4–3 late in regulation in Game 6, New York forward James Sheppard was assessed a delay-of-game penalty for shooting the puck over the Plexiglas. The officials huddled before deciding that the puck didn't touch the boards as it flew out of play.

Had New York coach Alain Vigneault had a challenge available, he would have used it and video would have shown that the puck did touch the boards as it exited the playing surface.

As it turned out, the Capitals didn't score on the power play. But had they scored and then won the game in overtime, that incorrect call could have cost the Rangers plenty.

By winning that game, the Rangers forced a Game 7 in their building. What's that worth to them? Probably $2.5 million or more. That's too much to lose simply because we are fearful of extending the average length of games by having too many reviews. There's too much at stake in today's game to let everything come down to what eight eyes saw on the ice. We need to use modern technology as much as possible to get it right.

Getting the calls right should be the objective over everything else.

Over the past couple of years, I've also become disenchanted with the number of crosschecks I'm seeing near the boards. I'm fearful we are going to end up with a player paralyzed because of an irresponsible hit too near the glass.

I would like to see the NHL experiment with the use of what is often called a "look-up line," which is a essentially a 40-inch orange warning track line that extends all the way around the rink to remind players when they are close to the boards.

A former Boston area junior player, Thomas Smith, has incredibly suffered two separate paralyzing injuries along the boards and has become a champion of having this line placed in every hockey rink. I saw it used in a prep school game and I believe it would have value at the NHL level.

Smith's lobbying efforts do not include an officiating component to the line's use. But that's where I believe it could really benefit the NHL.

Once a player reaches that line, he knows that he has entered an area in which a crosscheck or a hit from behind will result in a penalty and possible suspension. It would be easy for the Office of Player Safety to enforce, because officials can see clearly on video whether a player has crossed the orange line.

If the NHL started handing down two- or three-game suspensions without pay, it wouldn't take long to change the dangerous checking habits that today's players have. Nothing alters athlete behavior more than lost wages.

I also believe it's time to put an effort into actively recruiting former players from my generation to become involved in team management.

Unquestionably, I'm biased. But my generation of players was the best in NHL history. We were skilled, proud, and mentally tough. The NHL needs players from my generation to join the management teams of current NHL teams to offer some guidance.

As much as I enjoy today's game, I believe current players go down too easy, dive too much, and make a spectacle of themselves when they suffer any form of injury. Obviously, not everyone in the league is guilty. But there are enough guilty parties to warrant making a pronounced effort to change their behavior. If we don't do something, maybe we should add an acting coach to the NHL team's staffs.

We have too much drama in the game. Players throw off their gloves and act as if they are mortally wounded. They throw back their heads if a stick nicks them to make sure the referee sees it. We've become like soccer, where it is commonplace for players to act as if they are severely injured to sell a call. It's embarrassing. Former players from my generation need to remind today's players that you need to have some dignity even when you are injured.

I know this is politically incorrect to say, but we have too many pussies in the modern game.

Do you think a player would act like that if Mark Messier was his coach or Claude Lemieux was in a team's front office? If I had been successful in my bid to land a team in Seattle, Lemieux was going to be one of my first management hires.

Chelios works with young players in the Detroit Red Wings organization and I'm confident that if any of the players he is mentoring acted in that manner, he would not be shy about getting in their faces.

I don't see much overacting coming from Yzerman's team in Tampa Bay. We need to pull Wayne Gretzky back in the game, and I'm hoping Keith Tkachuk becomes more involved.

When Czech legend Jaromir Jagr turns 50 and finally retires, we need him to stay over here in the States and work in the front office of some team.

The final area where team managers need to alter their thinking is in their player signings. The decisions general managers are making on contracts today are mind-boggling.

As much as I appreciate the pressure they are under to stay competitive, I believe some of the contracts they have given out in recent years defy common sense.

How in the world could the Carolina Hurricanes give Alexander Semin $7 million per season over five seasons? Everyone in the NHL, including fans on Twitter, knew that was an ill-advised signing. His history showed that the consistency of his effort was not to be trusted.

Plus, Semin's situation was a distraction to his teammates. How do you think the Carolina players felt having him in the dressing room? He was hurting the team and everyone knew it because he lacked the drive to work hard every night.

I'm certainly not against players earning big money. I believe Jonathan Toews is worth every penny of his $10.5 million average salary. He is a proven, productive player who carries his team on and off the ice.

But what were the Florida Panthers thinking when they gave Dave Bolland a deal worth $5.5 million? They didn't owe him for scoring a Stanley Cup–winning goal for Chicago. He's a third-line center. You can't pay a third-liner that amount of money and not hurt the overall competitiveness of your team.

I love St. Louis Blues center Paul Stastny. I would want him on my team. He's a dependable, versatile, two-way center. He can help your team win in a variety of ways. But he is not a $7.5 million player.

You can't criticize the Chicago Blackhawks for the way they have handled their salary cap situation. General manager Stan Bowman has kept that team competitive, but even they have made contract mistakes. I would have to conclude that they regret giving Bryan Bickell $16 million over four years. He's a role player, not a top-six forward.

Teams can't keep making these poor decisions and then wonder why their teams aren't as successful as they would like them to be.

When I look around the NHL and see the decisions that are being made, I get more convinced that I could help an NHL team. I love working for NBC and the people in front of and behind the cameras are the best in the business. I will always be so grateful to the network for giving me a chance to talk about the game I love for a living. But one of my long-term goals is to find the right opportunity to become a decision-maker. It would seem like I would be a good fit for an expansion team, or a market that needs to connect more with fans. Most teams need people who know and understand the game, people who love it and are passionate about promoting it. You want people who enjoy being out in the community. You want people who enjoy walking through the arena concourse to meet fans. You want people who can spearhead a ticket drive. I can be effective in all those situations.

If I can borrow a term from my golf bag, I want to be a hybrid executive. I want to be a hybrid executive who can make decisions, work with young prospects, and also go into the community and sell tickets.

Calgary Flames president Brian Burke and Columbus Blue Jackets president John Davidson do have a pseudo-hybrid approach, but not to the extent I would. I want to be involved in player evaluation, player selection, player development, and franchise development. I want be in involved in putting together the roster, and I want to be the guy who stops by the suites before the game to say hello to our corporate sponsors. I want to be the guy who speaks to the Kiwanis Club and visits schools and makes phone calls to get the last few season-ticket holders we need.

I think I relate well with people, and I think it would make a difference if I set a day aside every week to connect with our ticket holders and sponsors.

No matter if we were winning or losing, I would be comfortable walking the concourses between periods.

If fans tell me our team stinks, and I agree with them, I will tell them that. I understand the fans' mentality.

If I was a team president and director of hockey operations, I would get on the ice at rookie camp and explain what our franchise was all about. During the season, I would go watch our top prospects and talk to them about our franchise's expectations for them. I would explain to them what it takes to be a successful NHL player.

Considering I scored 513 NHL regular-season goals and another 53 in the playoffs, I would hope I have some street cred with younger players.

I would be comfortable being the face of the team, the way Phil Esposito was in the early years in Tampa Bay. I would strive to be the NHL's most diverse executive.

If I were in charge of a team, I would be following the Detroit Red Wings' script. My emphasis would be heavy on scouting and player development. That's the primary reason why the Red Wings have made the playoffs for 24 consecutive seasons. They turn late-round picks into productive players. They develop depth. I love the Red Wings' development plan. They make sure they have the right coach in the American League, and then ask Chris Chelios to go down there and work with the younger players. They don't rush their prospects. Their general manager, Ken Holland, always says the Red Wings bring up their prospects when they are "overripe."

By the way, I want players who are comfortable dealing with the community. When you win over the fans in the community, you create a buzz about the hockey team. When there is a buzz about the team, the arena is electric. When the arena is electric, teams get charged up. When teams are charged up, they win.

My team would be a puck-possession and skating team. We would play physical. I've always loved the Philadelphia Flyers' tradition of making big hits. Fans expect that from players, and players want to become fan favorites so they hit even if they aren't normally hitters.

I'm not sure who I want to coach the team, but I believe I would be looking for a guy who has Jon Cooper's demeanor and approach and Joel Quenneville's experience and bench presence. When Quenneville walks up and down the bench, you can see the fire in his eyes. He gets animated on the bench. He shows you a full range of emotions. I believe players need to know there is a true boss, someone who holds them accountable. I think players want to play for Cooper because he's smart and genuine. He cares about his players, and that comes through. He makes sure everyone involved with the team feels like they matter. Players work hard for him because they don't want to disappoint him.

I want to be involved in building a championship team, including signing and developing players. I feel as if I have good instincts about who can play and who can't. No one can guarantee that they will never make a mistake assessing a player, but I'm confident that I will make fewer mistakes than are being made by teams today.

I would love the opportunity to help win the Stanley Cup that eluded me when I was a player. And I'd be happy to take a celebratory photo with our capable commissioner.

TEN

REGRETS

AP Images

CHAPTER TEN

Regrets

Sometimes I believe that three words, uttered in a moment of frustration, may have dramatically altered the course of my NHL career.

Near the end of the 1994–95 NHL season, a reporter asked me whether Darryl Sutter should return as coach of the Chicago Blackhawks.

"I don't care," I said.

In hindsight, those words may have been the unofficial start of the breakdown of my relationship with Blackhawks owner Bill Wirtz. The situation deteriorated to the point that I was traded to the Phoenix Coyotes the following year. Wirtz was a man who believed in loyalty, and I don't imagine he appreciated my lack of support for Sutter.

As a general rule, I don't live in a world full of regrets. If you make a mistake, you acknowledge it, apologize if appropriate, and move on. To be brutally honest, I don't have too many serious regrets in my life.

But I do regret not standing up for Darryl Sutter because he is one of my all-time favorite people in hockey.

What I should have said was, "He's a great coach. I like him a lot. I have a lot of respect for him. I hope he comes back."

That was the truth. So why didn't I say that? Because I'm an emotional guy and it is difficult for me to separate conflicting feelings when all of them seem connected.

It was approaching time for me to negotiate a new contract, and it was already evident that it was going to be a challenging road. Not long before I talked to the reporter, I had suffered a knee injury on a collision with Dallas Stars defenseman Derian Hatcher. Plus, Darryl and I butted heads all season over how I should play the game.

What I liked most about Darryl was that he was an old-school coach, similar to Mike Keenan. You knew where you stood with both Keenan and Sutter. They were straightforward in their approach. But Darryl and I couldn't agree on how I should be trying to score goals.

He believed I should be leading the physical charge in every minute of every game. I didn't believe we needed to play dump-and-chase hockey every time we entered the offensive zone.

Tension over this disagreement was frequent and intense. But as I've said many times, it's possible to have a major disagreement with a coach and still respect him.

I should have said all of that to the reporter. Instead, I went on local radio station WSCR and detailed the philosophical differences I had with Sutter. The *Chicago Tribune* characterized my position as, "[Roenick] would not be unhappy to see a new coach."

Sutter's contract was expiring at the end of that season, and he chose to resign for family reasons.

I don't believe my opinion had anything to do with Sutter's departure, but I do believe my lack of support for Sutter prompted management and ownership to see me in a different light. Instead of seeing me as a brash but valuable cornerstone, they may have started to see me as a potential troublemaker.

The biggest regret I have about my career is that I didn't work harder during that time to salvage my relationship with the Blackhawks. If I could have successfully completed a negotiation for a new contract in 1995, I might have ended up a Blackhawk for life.

The way the great fans of Chicago treat me today makes me realize that if I could have played there longer, I would be considered one of the top players in Blackhawks history.

I played eight seasons in Chicago and I'm treated like a favorite son when I return. When I did appearances for my first book, some people waited in line for two or three hours for my autograph.

I see how popular Bobby Hull, Stan Mikita, and Denis Savard are in that town, and I believe I could have a similar status if I would have re-signed with the Blackhawks in 1995. I might have my number hanging from the rafters had I scored my 513 NHL goals in a Blackhawks jersey.

As I have grown older and more experienced in the business world, I am far more sympathetic to Bill Wirtz's negotiation position than I was back then.

Eric Lindros' first contract with the Flyers had upped the price of poker, and most of the top players were receiving major raises as a result. My agent Neil Abbott told the Blackhawks I wanted between $4 and $5 million per season, depending on the length of the contract.

Wirtz said I wasn't worth that kind of money, and general manager Bob Pulford said I would never get a deal that would pay me $4 million per season.

Obviously those words angered me and I became more entrenched in my position.

Back then, I didn't know shit about the hockey business. I just knew that I was the team's drawing card, and I had averaged just under 50 goals per season for a three-year period from 1991–92 to 1993–94.

Wirtz's position was that the team's revenue didn't support paying me the kind of salary I was demanding.

Our position was that my demands fit into the new salary structure that had been established by the Lindros contract. Wirtz felt that just because other owners were jumping off a bridge didn't mean he had to jump with them. Salaries were doubling and tripling, and Wirtz believed the league's revenues didn't support that.

Now that I'm older, I can at least appreciate Wirtz's position. He had been a successful businessman for a long time, and he didn't believe that one contract should set the parameters for a completely new market. He believed that every team should be doing what was best for its bottom line.

Having made some tough business decisions myself, I understand why he tried to remain frugal at a time when player salaries were escalating dramatically. He viewed it as salaries escalating out of control.

Given what happened with the canceled season in 2004–05, maybe he was right.

I regret that I didn't work harder to find a compromise. To stay in Chicago, I probably would have had to accept a contract that was under market value. The Blackhawks were offering $3 million per season and I ended up getting my $4 million per season from the Phoenix Coyotes after I was traded.

To stay in Chicago, I probably would have also had to agree to start keeping my mouth shut. I would have had to be a puppet. I don't know if I could have done that. But it might have been worth giving that a try. I missed Chicago as soon as I left.

In hindsight, maybe my best course of action was to push for all of the money I could get. But undoubtedly my mouth put me in more jeopardy with the Blackhawks than my salary demands. I think the Wirtz family viewed me as a live hand grenade with the pin already halfway out.

Here are some other regrets I have about my career:

Going from East to West

When Philadelphia Flyers general manager Bobby Clarke asked me to waive my no-trade clause to facilitate a move to the Los Angeles Kings, I should have politely declined.

It was a mistake for me to leave Philadelphia, where fans appreciated how I played the game.

I enjoyed playing in a city where they appreciated intensity as much as scoring goals. If you play hockey like you are the Tasmanian Devil, Philadelphia fans will love you to death.

My decision to waive my no-trade clause was born out of a mixture of hurt and anger.

When the Blackhawks traded me on August 16, 1996, it was the first time any team had ever said, "We don't want you anymore, J.R." The second time was when Clarke called me.

You feel disappointed. You feel wounded. You feel shunned.

The Flyers wanted to trade me to clear salary cap space for the acquisition of Peter Forsberg. At the time, I was making $4.94 million. I understood their interest in Forsberg, who was one of the NHL's best all-around forwards. He was younger than me, and I was coming off a concussion. I understood why it made sense for the Flyers.

Still, in my last season in Philadelphia, I scored 19 goals in 62 games. That's essentially a 25-goal season. In the playoffs, I totaled 13 points in 18 games. Based on those numbers, didn't I deserve to be brought back?

In hindsight, I didn't handle the rejection well. My immediate reaction was that if the Flyers didn't want me, then I didn't want them. I should have fought more aggressively to stay where I was.

My worst NHL performance

It's easy to identify the worst game I ever played: it was Game 2 of the 1992 Stanley Cup Final, when the Chicago Blackhawks lost to the Pittsburgh Penguins.

We had suffered a devastating loss in Game 1, blowing a 4–1 lead to lose 5–4. That was the game when Jaromir Jagr weaved through our entire team to score the tying goal with less than five minutes left in regulation. That has to be one of the most spectacular goals in NHL history. Mario Lemieux scored the game-winner with 13 seconds left.

As a younger player, I didn't know how to cope with that level of disappointment. We owned an 11-game winning streak coming into that game. We felt invincible. Some of the veteran guys in the Blackhawks dressing room were reminding us not to let one game ruin our series, but I was so low after that game that I couldn't dig myself out. I didn't sleep the night before Game 2.

I played so poorly that coach Mike Keenan benched me, along with my linemates Michel Goulet and Steve Larmer, in the second period.

It was clearly my fault. I was ineffective to the point that I brought down the entire line. I felt as if I was skating in quicksand. My legs wouldn't move. I made bad decisions. I was throwing pucks in the middle of the ice. I remember Larmer yelling at me constantly because I was embarrassingly out of sync.

That's how we operated on the Blackhawks. When someone played poorly, you got in his face.

I don't know if we would have won the series if I had played better in Game 2, but I would have loved to have seen what we could have done if I had produced one of my best games.

A weighty problem

After the cancellation of the 2004–05 season because of the lockout, the NHL was scheduled to restart in September of 2005.

I scheduled a vacation to Italy that began August 28.

That's the same Italy where you spend many hours of many days stuffing your face with pasta and bread, and your gullet is coated in Barolo wine. It's an orgy of food and drink.

What the hell was I thinking? I was 35 years old and had missed a season of competition. I should have been pouring my heart into a conditioning regimen, not pouring another glass of red.

When I returned from Italy, I had roughly 48 hours to prepare for training camp. I spent my first day skating and my second day in the gym. It didn't help. When I showed up at camp, I was a bloated 220 pounds. I have never felt sicker than I did after I skated in the first day of that training camp.

I was told I had to lose 18 pounds, and I can tell you it didn't come off easily. The length of time it took to shed the weight made the coaching staff even more unhappy.

The decision to take that vacation was among the worst decisions of my career. By going abroad when I did, I set myself up for failure in Los Angeles.

My only defense is that I didn't really believe we were going to play in 2005–06 when I planned that vacation. But I should have planned as if we were going to play. I knew better.

The other issue was that I was still experiencing concussion symptoms long after I left Philadelphia, and I wasn't able to maintain any level of conditioning during the lost season. When I joined the Kings, I felt like I was trying to transform myself from couch potato to elite athlete.

What I needed was a teammate to push me. That always works better than being yelled at by coaches. That's why I always missed having friends such as Keith "Walt" Tkachuk and Chris Chelios on my team.

If I needed to be chewed out, those guys wasted no time getting in my face. Chelios still does it. When I packed on too much weight after I retired, Chelios constantly pestered me to get my act together. That man is a freak. He weighs 183 pounds, the same weight he played at in his first season in Montreal. When I started doing a new training regimen as part of an NBC promotion, Chelios called me and said, "It's about time."

Tkachuk and Chelios tell it like it is because they care about me. But when I joined the Kings, there was nobody there pushing me except the coaches. To be honest, I believe teammates were afraid to get on me because they thought I might fly off the handle. I have that reputation.

Most guys are aware that I can be explosive. If I think you are pushing my buttons for no good reason, or if I feel you are being disloyal, I can pull the curtain on you. Once I do that, you are not getting back into my inner circle. I can be cruel.

It took me six or seven weeks to get in shape, and I never fully felt like I regained my stride in Los Angeles. That vacation in Italy cost me my opportunity to succeed with the Kings. It was an epic mistake.

Missed opportunities

If I could have played for another American-based team during my career, my first choice would be the New York Rangers.

Seeing how the city responded to Mark Messier, I think I would have bonded with the fans in the Big Apple. It's likely that I would have appeared too often in the *New York Post* gossip pages. I definitely would have done the David Letterman show. But I would have enjoyed playing in New York, where the spotlight and nightlife burn bright.

I also believe I missed out by not playing in Canada. As most of my fans know, I love Canada's passion for our sport. I regret not playing at least one season for a Canadian NHL team. When Darryl Sutter was general manager in Calgary, I talked to him about playing for the Flames. I always believed I would have loved playing there. I love Calgary's fans. They always treated me well in that city.

But the Canadian team I would have loved to play for is the Toronto Maple Leafs.

While watching Phil Kessel get eaten alive by the Toronto media, I kept thinking that I would have loved all of the attention that Phil was trying to avoid.

Throughout my career, I have enjoyed a strong relationship with the media, and I don't believe that would have changed in Toronto. I regret not having the chance to see if I could have owned that city. As cocky as I can be, you know I believe I would have had the media eating out of my hand.

This is how you treat your friends?

I've seen Tony Amonte many times since my first book was published and he has never mentioned what I had to say about the time I cut him up with stick in a game in Chicago.

If you recall, I was enraged by my wife calling me out of the Coyotes dressing room between periods to confront me about how much I had changed as a person. She said my life was spiraling out of control because of my gambling and the people I had picked as my new friends.

As my teammates looked on, Tracy told me that I had to change because I was destroying our family. Our heated argument spilled out of the intermission and into the third period. Finally, Tracy screamed "I'm out of here" and stalked off.

When I hit the ice, I was in a blind rage and someone was going to pay a price. I was going to hurt someone. It turned out to be my childhood friend, Tony.

There were many wild stories about what had happened that night, but the truth was that I was blinded by anger to the point that I didn't even know who I was attacking. Whether Amonte believes that or not I don't know, but that is the truth.

I'm not surprised that he has not brought up the event. That's his way. Tony was called to be interviewed for my first book. He chose not to respond.

It's his way to let sleeping dogs lie. He's not a guy who wants to sit down and hash out his feelings. I've never joined hands with Tony and sung "Kumbaya." It feels like we still have a friendship, but I can feel that there is a wedge between us.

My level of respect for Tony has never changed. If I ever get in a position to manage an NHL team, Amonte is one person I would attempt to hire. This is a guy who knows and understands what it takes to be successful in the NHL. He was a small player who not only survived but thrived in the NHL.

Unquestionably, I wish I never cut him.

One other regret I have is that I could never be friends with fellow American Derian Hatcher. If you recall, Hatcher broke my jaw with an elbow in 1999, less than three weeks after I had knocked out his Dallas Stars teammate Mike Modano with what was deemed a borderline late hit.

The 240-pound Hatcher caught me with an elbow along the boards after I skated behind the net. The sound my jaw made as it was blown apart by Hatcher's strength was like the sound you hear when ice cracks beneath your feet. It gives me shivers to remember that sound. He was suspended seven games for what would have been considered assault and battery if it happened on the street. With my jaw wired shut, I lost 17 pounds, but I played in a playoff game 16 days later.

Let me be clear about this: had I been given an opportunity, I would have broken Hatcher's jaw or ankle. I wanted revenge. I would have hated myself for doing it, but I would have tried to hurt him the way he hurt me. That is just part of the eye-for-an-eye, tooth-for-a-tooth hockey code of justice.

But what I really regret is that the incident meant we could never be friends. The truth is I admired the way Hatcher played. I could relate to the physical force he used to be an effective player. He played the game the way I believed the game should be played. He would tell you that he was standing up for Modano when he rearranged my face.

Had we played on the same NHL team, we probably would have been friends. But we were never friends when we played together on U.S. national teams. We showed no outward animosity toward each other—I even told Hatcher that I didn't hate him for what he did—but we were never close. We didn't sit next to each other in the locker room. We didn't go out to dinner together. He was not going to invite me boating in his native Michigan and I wasn't going to invite him out to Arizona to play golf.

I admired him for being the first American captain to win a Stanley Cup. I was also envious. I wish I didn't have the resentment I had for him. But that is what can happen in the NHL. It's not a game for people whose feelings—or bones—are damaged easily.

The worst bet of my life

When I was in the midst of my degenerate gambling period, roughly 14 years ago, I was regularly paying $1,000 to a handicapper just for betting tips.

He would call me up and sell me on his sure bet of the night. He always professed to have inside information about injuries, or who was in the coach's doghouse, or who was about to become a starter, or who was about to soar.

One day this guy called me and said I needed to bet big on Long Island University's men's basketball team against Manhattan College. He said Long Island was getting six points, and my handicapper was convinced Long Island was going to win the game. It was the second game of the season and he said no one appreciated how good Long Island was. As I recall, the handicapper also said Manhattan was dealing with injuries.

Before that night, I had never heard of Long Island University or Manhattan College. They could have been high school teams for all I knew. But I didn't care—that's how far down the rabbit hole I was when it came to gambling.

Being an amateur gambling idiot at that point, I not only laid a bet on Long Island but parlayed it with every other team playing that night. That means if Kentucky played Duke that night, I took a parlay bet with both Long Island and Kentucky winning and another bet with Long Island and Duke winning.

As I recall, there were 30 games that night, meaning I had 60 parlay bets with Long Island being one of the winning teams. Because I knew Long Island was going to win, I knew I would make enough on my 30 winners to make it a very profitable night.

The only problem was that Manhattan steamrolled Long Island. Final score: 111–84. My losses that night were more than $60,000.

That was the night I began to realize that my handicapper was only selling me his dream of becoming rich off my gambling habit. His business strategy was to tout both sides of a bet to assure that half of his clients were happy every night. In other words, my guy sold me on Long Island, but if I had called him 10 minutes later, he would have sold me on Manhattan.

By the way, Long Island University started that season by losing 16 in a row. Manhattan started the season by winning 12 of its first 13.

I regret ever talking to a handicapper. I could have stopped any two drunks at a bar and received better betting information than I was receiving from my paid handicappers.

Adult programming

It is one thing to be an adult, but it's another thing to act like one. One of my biggest regrets was not understanding how to act responsibly when I first became an NHL player.

Once I turned pro, I was J.R. gone wild. The straight-laced kid from high school became the gambler and party guy.

I was unprepared for stardom. I was unprepared for my celebrity status. I was unprepared to deal with the wealth I had. I was a teenager making more than my father. I wasn't prepared for that. I made poor decisions. I didn't put my family first. You could say I had a God complex, because I felt I was always right. I wouldn't listen to anyone, including Tracy, who knew that I was hanging out with the wrong people and traveling down the wrong path. It wasn't as if I became a monster, but I was transformed into another person. I wasn't the same person after I became a star. When I look back now, I don't even recognize the guy I became in my first few seasons in the NHL.

I regret that I didn't appreciate what I had until much later in my career.

ELEVEN

TWO PARTS WELLS, ONE PART BARKLEY, AND A DASH OF URLACHER

CHAPTER ELEVEN

Two Parts Wells, One Part Barkley, and a Dash of Urlacher

Wayne Gretzky has been around professional hockey since 1978, and I don't believe he has ever uttered a word that has landed him in really hot water.

Even when the Great One called the New Jersey Devils a "Mickey Mouse organization" in 1983, I suspect most of the people within the world of hockey were thankful that someone finally had the courage to tell the Devils to get their act together.

My buddy Gretzky has always delivered the right words at the right time. He is consistently classy and always respectful of the game. He routinely puts the game in a favorable light. He is a model citizen, a bastion of political correctness and positive attitudes. He is a pillar of the hockey community.

I could not possibly have more respect for Gretzky. I admire him more than anyone else in hockey.

But I could never be like him. I wouldn't even know how.

I don't have the same filters on my brain that Wayne possesses. He always seems to know when the wisest thing to do is to say nothing. It never occurs to me not to say anything.

I am often entertaining, occasionally politically incorrect, and often outside the box in my thinking. That's who I am. If you want me in your life, you have to accept that sometimes trouble comes galloping out of my mouth like the Charge of the Light Brigade.

Unquestionably, players should conduct themselves more like Gretzky and less like I do. But I do believe hockey needs colorful athletes to keep the game fresh and appealing. First and foremost, you need talented players to keep fans interested, but you also need memorable characters.

Brett Hull and I were similar because we could both score goals and work a room like we were hosting an open mic at a comedy club. But Hull is more sarcastic and opts for droll humor more than I do. Hull doesn't enjoy dancing in the spotlight as much as I do.

I identify with athletes from other sports more often than I do with other hockey players.

Here is a list of some of the athletes, all of whom I consider friends, whose styles remind me of my own:

U.S. skier Bode Miller

When I got to know Bode well at the 2002 Winter Olympics, I felt like he was to skiing what I was to hockey.

As an athlete, he was daring and willing to do anything to win. I played with reckless abandon on and off the ice, and he showed reckless abandon on the slopes and in his private life.

He wasn't afraid to say whatever was on his mind. Miller didn't pull his punches when he spoke to the media. He has flair, a presence about him, and he loved competing for his country.

He quickly became one of my favorite athletes. If Miller played hockey, I believe he would have played the game the way I did. He would have been a top-line center who wasn't timid about flattening his opponents.

U.S. speed skater Dan Jansen

Jansen is one of the nicest athletes I've ever met, which is something I really admire.

He treats everyone he meets with a high level of respect, which I have also tried to do throughout my career in sports.

I've always been fascinated with Jansen's blend of power and grace on the ice. One reason why I was always envious of NHL star Mike Modano was the blend of power and grace he owned as a skater. Jansen, the 1994 Olympic gold medalist at 1,000 meters, had that same combination.

He was explosive and churned around the oval at a high rate of speed but made it look like he wasn't working hard. He made skating look easy, and I can tell you from experience that it isn't.

Pitcher David Wells

I am good friends with Wells, a fact I'm sure doesn't surprise you.

Wells was a super-charged athlete who partied like a rock star. In his 2003 autobiography, *Perfect I'm Not*, Wells insisted that he was "half drunk" and nursing a "raging, skull-rattling hangover" when he pitched a perfect game. He wrote that he climbed into bed at 5:00 AM, slept for an hour, then threw Major League Baseball's 15th perfect game that evening.

The left-hander has a tattoo of Babe Ruth on his pitching arm. Considering my own tattoo history, you know I appreciate that.

Wells once secured a cap worn by Ruth and then donned it while pitching in a major league game. How cool is that?

This man knows more famous people than anyone else in this universe or the next. He's a fun-loving, humorous, adventurous human being who happened to have enough athletic ability to win 239 major league games.

Boomer was a bulldog on the mound. If you were crowding the plate, you were going to find a fastball zooming under your chin. If you dared stare back at him, or say something to him about his purpose pitch, he would just laugh in your face.

That's obviously similar to how I played hockey. If I caught you coming around the net with your head down, I was going to try to take your head off your shoulders. Boomer and I were kindred spirits in that regard.

I loved the way he competed and refused to allow his sport to dictate how he lived his life. He doesn't give a fuck what comes out of his mouth. If you don't like it, that's too bad.

Linebacker Brian Urlacher

When he played linebacker for the Chicago Bears, staring into Urlacher's face mask was like looking into the face of death. His eyes told you that he was more physical than you were. His eyes told you that he wanted to knock your teeth out.

Obviously I was not as physically imposing as Urlacher, but I had his mentality when I played in the NHL. In my mind, I had the same menacing look on my face. I believe I made it clear that I could cause you pain if given the opportunity. When I was whirling around the ice like a category 4 hurricane, I could tell that opposing players didn't want to be caught in my path. I may not have been 6-foot-3 or 220 pounds, but I could skate fast enough to make you feel like you had been in a car crash when I hit you.

I identified with the intensity that Urlacher brought to the NFL. I became friends with him over time and I believe he respected the ferocity I brought to my sport.

Hockey player Cammi Granato

I loved watching Cammi play because she was such an intense competitor. She wasn't always the most talented player on the ice, but she always got the most out of her ability by playing with a burning desire.

She typified the Granato family tradition of always playing every game like they had something to prove. Her brother Tony was a smaller player who played big. He was a Jeep who performed like a tank.

Cammi had that same kind of grit. When I watched her wheel around the ice, I thought she had the same level of desire that I had carried around.

NBA legend Charles Barkley

The first night I met Barkley, we closed down the Excalibur bar in Chicago together like we were a couple of old army buddies. The tavern's staff almost had to push us out the door.

He's irreverent, to be sure, but he's an affable, kind-hearted man who lights up a room with his energy. If you want to have the world's best dinner party, you would want Barkley at the table.

Years ago, Barkley, in Chicago to play against the Bulls, decided to attend a Chicago Blackhawks game. He became fascinated by how I played the game and decided to come down to our dressing room to meet me.

"Where's that Roenick kid?" he bellowed as he entered the room.

He stood in front of me and said that the way I played hockey reminded him of the way he played basketball. He said he loved my aggressiveness. I always say it was one of the best compliments I ever received because Barkley was a beast on the NBA hardwood.

I invited him to shoot pool with us after the game and we've been friends ever since. We have a great time together. He likes to flirt with Tracy, and he pals around with my son, Brett.

We always have plenty to talk about. For example, when we flew home together from the Lake Tahoe Celebrity Golf Tournament in July of 2015, we commiserated about how challenging it is to be a television analyst in the age of social media.

It drives us both crazy that fans tell us they love hearing us give our honest, unfiltered options, then unleash the hounds on us as soon as we are critical about their team.

The one difference between Charles and me is that he won't even look at social media. I go on social media all the time and get myself in trouble. Maybe Charles has the right idea.

Golfer Ian Poulter

Fred Couples is my favorite golfer, and I wish I had his temperament on the golf course.

A former Masters champion, he has a very carefree, laid-back attitude when he is playing. Nothing seems to bother him. When he makes an errant shot, he shrugs and moves on. I'm the opposite. When I make a poor shot, I'm far from laid-back. I go immediately to DEFCON 1. Ready the silos. The missiles are about to launch.

When I golf, I feel like I'm attacking the ball. Meanwhile, Couples takes this gorgeous, effortless swing and the ball rockets down the fairway with greater distance than I can muster by swinging with all of my might.

I've tried to learn by watching Couples, but me copying his approach is like a Type A business executive trying to work meditation into his workday.

The golfer that I truly resemble in style is England's Ian Poulter. I've seen him try to murder the ground with his club after making a bad shot. Go on YouTube and you will find videos of Poulter beating Mother Earth after missing the green with a short pitch. I've seen him boil over after coming up short with a wedge in his hand. In other words, I've seen him perform my act on the golf course.

He will engage hecklers. He has a wild streak in him. He's a guy who can get himself in trouble on Twitter. Poulter is my kind of guy.

Couples is a congenial man and a great hockey fan. When this book was being written, I ran into him and his first question was, "J.R., what happened to Seattle getting an NHL team?"

"Fred, I think you and I should try to get a group together to get a team up there," I said.

"That would be great," Couples said. "Call me and we will see what we can do together."

Working with Couples on a business project would be like asking Frank Sinatra and Mick Jagger to write a song together. While their styles may be dramatically different, you know whatever they produced would be worth listening to.

Couples and I could make a fascinating team. Honestly though, I don't know which would make me happier—Couples helping me put together a group of millionaires to land a team in Seattle, or him helping me discover a path to a calmer, more stress-free golf game.

TWELVE

BENNY AND THE JET

CHAPTER TWELVE

Benny and the Jet

Dan Quayle spent four years as vice president of the United States, and one night watching me having a tramp stamp inked on my lower back at a tattoo parlor in Palm Springs, California.

This was one of those crazy nights you had to be there to fully appreciate. But I'll describe it for you the best I can.

The story starts in 1996 after I became friends with Quayle, who lived around the corner from me in the Finisterre gated community in Paradise Valley, Arizona. Quayle and I were primarily golfing buddies, but my wife was close enough to Dan and his wife, Marilyn, to be invited to accompany them on a two-week safari-like excursion to the African bush.

On that trip, the former Veep suffered what local guides called a "worm" bite, which comes with complications.

The bite resulted in Quayle breaking out with a hideous, itchy rash on his chest that caused him considerable discomfort. He was forced to smear medicinal cream on his hairy chest every night. Somehow, seeing that nightly process prompted Tracy to stick Dan with the nickname "Hairy Worm." Committed to keeping the joke alive, she continued to use that nickname after we returned stateside.

Through my friendship with Quayle, I was privy to some excellent golfing opportunities. He introduced me to Tim Blixseth, a timber baron who was once listed by *Forbes* as one of the nation's wealthiest men. This was more than a decade ago and Blixseth has since taken blows to his bottom line, but back then he had a memorable golf course named Porcupine Creek in Palm Springs.

It was a phenomenal golfing experience. Porcupine Creek boasted six holes that made you feel as if you were golfing in the desert, six holes that made you feel like as if you were in the Colorado Rockies, and six more that it made it feel as if you were walking up fairways in Hawaii.

Dan called and asked if I wanted to play Creek in a tournament that would feature many top businessmen Blixseth knew.

I jumped at the opportunity and then asked whether my former Chicago Blackhawks teammate Stephan Matteau could tag along as my wingman. The always-accommodating Quayle said to bring him along. We flew there on Quayle's jet.

Quayle often brought his son, Ben, then in his early twenties, to the golf tournaments when I was involved. Quayle particularly liked to golf in the Lake Tahoe Celebrity Tournament, and when he was there, he would essentially leave Ben in my custody.

"I'm too old, I have to go to sleep," Dan would joke to his son. "You go hang out with J.R. I know you will have fun with him."

One of my favorite memories of the Porcupine Creek event was celebrating Ben's first hole-in-one. It was fun for me to watch Ben Quayle grow up to be a U.S. congressman in Arizona. He had to defeat 10 fellow Republicans in the primary to get elected in 2010. Unfortunately, redistricting forced him to face another sitting congressman in the next election. He lost to David Schweikert 53 percent to 47 percent in the primary.

Before he left the House, the younger Quayle was judged to be the most conservative member of that chamber by the *National Journal.* I would like to believe it was hearing my views on the news during our late-night partying and politicking sessions that steered him in that direction. It was more likely thanks to his father's guidance.

Both of the Quayle men always exercised good judgment when they were with me, like the night they chose to be spectators, rather than participants, as Matteau and I capped a night of golfing and drinking with a trip to the tattoo studio.

(By the way, it is never a good idea to make decisions about tattoos at 2:00 in the morning. It's better to make your tattoo commitment at 2:00 in the afternoon, when you are fully functional and alcohol-free. But you probably already knew that.)

Matteau at least had the good sense to have a tattoo of his children inked onto his arm.

My decision was to go with the tramp stamp. At least it says "My Angel," which is what I call Tracy. But I have to be honest and say it's a highly feminine-looking piece of art.

The next morning, when I made contact with Matteau, he asked, "What the fuck did we do last night?"

"We hung out with the former vice president of the United States, got hammered, and then got tattoos," I said.

Quayle and his son both seemed quite amused by our antics.

We were scheduled to fly back to Arizona from Palm Springs on a commercial airline, but Sunday morning, before we teed off,

Quayle said he was working on upgrading our transportation back to Arizona.

Later in the day, Quayle told me to cancel our other reservations. "We are catching a ride with my buddy," he said.

When we showed up at the commuter airport, we were escorted immediately to the tarmac. There, we found a private jet surrounded by guards armed with machine guns. Suddenly, we were being frisked, and wands were run over our bodies. Our identification was checked and rechecked. They asked questions that you wouldn't normally hear at airport security.

"Have you ever been to Israel or an Arab country?" the man asked me. "Have you ever been arrested? Affiliated with any political groups based outside of America?"

This is not the line of questioning you hear on your TSA security walk-through in American airports. These guys were not looking to see if I was trying to sneak bottled water or an extra-large shampoo onto the plane.

"What the hell is going on?" Matteau asked me after our interrogation was completed.

"I have no idea," I said.

Finally, we were allowed to board, and Quayle brought us over to meet his friend.

"Guys, this is my friend Benny," he said.

We shook hands and I thanked him for the ride. We made polite conversation about the golf course we had just played. Later, I found the right moment to pull Quayle aside and ask, "Why is this plane full of guys with guns?"

"Because Benny is the prime minister of Israel. It's Benjamin Netanyahu," he said, laughing.

Although I had not recognized Netanyahu, I knew enough about Middle East politics to appreciate that I was traveling with a man who was a primary target for multiple terrorist groups around the world. Counting the security force, there were about a dozen people on the plane.

The flight from Palm Springs was only an hour in length, but it was long enough for my imagination to run wild. It wasn't hard to picture terrorists taking down a jet with a rocket-propelled grenade.

But Netanyahu could not have been more gracious. World affairs never came up during our conversation. Mostly, we talked about golf. With all that he has to worry about on a daily basis, he probably didn't mind reliving all of his shots at Porcupine Creek for us, expressing the same enjoyment and frustration that the rest of us experienced on the challenging course.

Now, every time I see Netanyahu in the news I think about the short flight from Palm Springs to Arizona that seemed like an eternity because I was convinced the jet would be downed by some terrorist act.

Since I moved from Arizona to San Diego, we don't see the Quayles as often. But I still have the utmost respect for the man. He is chairman of global investments for Cerberus Capital Management, and he has friends on both sides of the aisle. Democrats and Republicans both like the man. He's witty, charming, and exceptionally sharp, although you wouldn't know that considering the way he was portrayed by the media.

One of my favorite Quayle memories was going to his house for an Election Night celebration in 2004. It was like a Super Bowl party, except the home team was the Republicans.

As winners and losers were announced, Dan and his friends would be yelling at the television screen just like a sports fan does on Super Bowl Sunday. That night, a room full of people were cheering on the Republicans like they were their favorite NFL team. Dan analyzed the election results with the same energy that a football fan would digest his team's play calling.

There was cheering, cursing, complaining, eating, and drinking. That was the night I realized that politics is a lot like sports, except the consequences of winning and losing has a far greater impact. Some sports fans would probably choose to disagree.

THIRTEEN

THE NUMBERS GAME

CHAPTER THIRTEEN

The Numbers Game

I never gave jersey numbers a moment's thought when I was a younger player, except for when I wondered why the fuck my speedy linemate Tony Amonte wore a defenseman's No. 3 at Thayer Academy.

People ask me why I wore No. 20 at Thayer, and the honest answer is because that's the number they gave me.

I wasn't the guy who lobbied or fought for the right to wear a specific number. I wanted whatever jersey fit my skinny ass. I wore 15 as a soccer player. I would have been equally happy to wear 16 or 18 or 22. I didn't need to wear No. 9 because it was a scorer's number. I didn't need to wear a number that some other athlete had made famous. A number didn't make me. I made the number. That's the way I looked at it.

The Chicago Blackhawks gave me No. 51 at my first training camp, and I would have been happy to wear that number the rest of my career if that's what the equipment men asked me to do. I was focused far more on the logo on the front of the jersey than I was the number on the back of it.

It was the fans who made me view my number as being important, because many of them want me to attach my number to my autograph. You realize quickly that your number is part of who you are to your fans. Even today, I sign photographs with my number. It feels as if you are adding your trademark, or personal logo, at the end of your name.

Players in general take jersey numbers quite seriously. When I was traded to the Phoenix Coyotes, one of the team's most popular players was Teppo Numminen, who happened to wear No. 27.

When I showed up, he pulled me aside and said that he would switch numbers to allow me to wear No. 27.

It was an incredibly classy gesture, but I declined his offer.

"You have earned your respect here and that's your number," I told him. "I'm the one making a change here, and I will change my number."

I opted to wear No. 97 because 1997 was the year my son was born. My production was roughly the same in my first season in Phoenix as it was in my last season in Chicago. I don't believe switching numbers caused any harm to my career.

But I respect the fact that other players do care greatly about their number. Even though Amonte wore a number that is associated with a plodding defenseman when he was in high school, he grew to love wearing No. 10 in the NHL when he was in Chicago. When he showed up in Philadelphia, John LeClair was already wearing No. 10. LeClair was a three-time 50-goal scorer wearing that number. Tony opted to get as close as he could to No. 10 by wearing No. 11. But it seemed challenging for him to make the switch. It did look odd seeing him wear No. 11.

The number switch that did have meaning to me occurred when I made the decision to return to wearing No. 27 in San Jose in 2007.

When I had worn No. 97, I had been one of the game's stars. But by 2007, the game and Father Time had humbled me. I wanted to symbolically show that I was willing to just be a contributor, not a star, in San Jose, doing whatever I could to help my team.

When I informed general manager Doug Wilson of my intentions, he laughed and said he had been thinking about asking me to make that switch. Both of us agreed that we needed to say good-bye to J.R. the superstar and reintroduce ourselves to Jeremy Roenick, the hard-working third-liner.

I would be lying if I said my jersey numbers are not important to me now that I'm retired. I enjoy signing the photographs with my number. It brings back fond memories. When you write down your number, it reminds you that there are still many fans in Chicago who have a No. 27 sweater hanging in their closet. There are folks in Philadelphia who still wear a No. 97 Roenick sweater to games.

More importantly, my son, Brett, now wears my No. 27 when he plays. That makes the number far more important to me than it did when I was wearing it.

In honor of my No. 27, here are the top 27 highlights of my hockey life:

1. Team USA beating the Soviet Union at the 1980 Olympics in Lake Placid

This game had a major influence on me wanting to become an Olympian and an NHL player. The memory of Mike Eruzione's game-winning goal and broadcaster Al Michaels' "Do you believe in miracles?" is forever ingrained in my memory. After watching the inspirational American performance, I wanted to be the next

Mike Eruzione. After I watched the Americans pull off the greatest upset in sports history, no one was going to stop me from being an elite hockey player.

I was preparing to play a youth league game that night in February of 1980 and I remember pulling on my uniform in the front room, in front of the television set. We watched the celebration on the ice and then ran to the car in our skates.

Believe it or not, watching Eruzione score fueled my hockey desire even more than watching Stanley Cup celebrations.

2. Earning an Olympic silver medal in 2002

It's been said that it takes years to become proud of winning a silver medal, because it's a reminder that you lost the gold medal game.

But I was proud of my silver medal the instant I received it. I didn't want to lose that gold medal game against Canada. The loss was devastating. However, owning an Olympic medal means the world to me. A medal of any color is an accomplishment.

Plus, I appreciate how far the American program has come in my lifetime. It doesn't take a miracle for the Americans to compete with anyone. We are a superpower in hockey, and the silver medal reminds me of that. When Americans show up at a tournament, we expect to win. My generation of American players helped cultivate that culture of success.

3. Winning back-to-back bantam national championships in 1983 and 1984

I was living in northern Virginia and commuting every weekend to Newark on People's Express Airlines to play with the New Jersey Rockets.

In the first year, we beat a quality Chicago Americans team 3–2 in quadruple overtime to win the title. I played that game with a separated shoulder against a Chicago team that boasted Justin Duberman, who ended up playing briefly for Pittsburgh, plus Eddie Olczyk's brother Rick and Joe Suk, who ended up playing in the Quebec Major Junior League.

The following season Duberman joined the Rockets and we defeated Detroit Compuware to win the title. Future NHL player Denny Felsner was on that squad.

By traveling every weekend to play at a high level, I began to understand the sacrifice and commitment that was a requirement to be successful in this sport.

4. Advancing to the 1992 Stanley Cup Final

I can put this on my list of worst moments as well, because my Blackhawks lost to the Pittsburgh Penguins.

At the time, I never would have guessed that it would be my only trip to the Stanley Cup Final.

Going into that series, we had won 11 consecutive games. I felt as if we should have been the favorite. It's almost forgotten now that we held a 4–1 lead in Game 1. But eventually Mario Lemieux and Jaromir Jagr took over the game and the series.

Still, when I look back, I'm glad I can say that I made it to the big dance. The Penguins gave us a lesson on what it takes to be a champion.

5. Watching the 1987 Canada Cup game between Canada and Russia

At 17, I was dreaming of being an NHL player. To see Wayne Gretzky and Mario Lemieux playing together for Canada against the Soviet Union couldn't have been more inspirational. Was that Canada Cup the greatest display of hockey ever? Watching Wayne and Mario collaborate on Lemieux's great goal was like a religious experience.

To watch this tournament on television the year before I was drafted showed me how driven you must be to develop into one of the best players in the game.

6. Playing in Moscow in 1987

I played for Team USA at the World Championships before the Berlin Wall fell in 1989. We didn't play well as a team, but the competition was incredible and the experience was mind-blowing. Nothing makes you appreciate life in America more than spending time in an oppressed country.

7. Becoming an All-Star in 1991

Does it get any better than playing your first All-Star Game in your home city? I was 21 and almost won the MVP award of the game in Chicago, posting a goal and two assists. Vincent Damphouse scored two late goals to win the balloting. The other thing I remember from that game was sitting next to Gretzky in the dressing room.

That day was exhilarating and nerve-racking for me at the same time. I wanted to make the game memorable for the hometown fans.

8. Scoring my first NHL goal

On Valentine's Day in 1989, I scored my first NHL goal against Minnesota North Stars goalie Kari Takko.

Coincidentally, the other Blackhawks player involved in the play was Brian Noonan, a Boston-area player who had played with me in a multitude of summer-league hockey games.

I had tried to pass the puck to Noonan but it bounced off his stick and into the goal crease. I darted in and shoveled the puck past Takko for the first of my 513 regular-season goals. After being recalled by Chicago, I had nine goals and nine assists for 18 points in the next 17 games. My career was officially launched.

9. Being drafted No. 8 overall in 1988

When the Blackhawks drafted me, it felt as if I had just won the lottery. In those days, most NHL teams still had more faith in Canadian junior players than they had in Americans. Plus, I only weighed 155 pounds. In that era, scouts were afraid of smaller players.

The NHL had such an intense focus on weight that my agent Neil Abbott wouldn't even let anyone weigh me that season. "The scale is not your friend," Neil would tell me.

Abbott's plan was to make my weight the biggest mystery of the draft. Scouts knew that Mike Modano was 6-foot-3, 212 pounds, and that Trevor Linden was 6-foot-4, 210 pounds. But no one was sure how much I weighed.

Abbott's plan worked to perfection. When the Blackhawks drafted me, the *Chicago Tribune* story said I weighed 179 pounds. I would have needed to have bowling balls in my pockets to tip the scale at 179.

Legend has it that Chicago assistant general manager Jack Davidson said at a pre-draft meeting that he would quit if the Blackhawks didn't draft me.

All I know is that being drafted eighth overall by an Original Six team in the Montreal Forum was one of the most emotional days of my life.

10. Joining the NHL's 500-goal club

When you are closing in on 500 career goals, your hope is that the milestone moment will come on a breakaway, with fans rising to their feet as you pull off a dramatic backhand-forehand move. You want it to be a game-winner, or at least a goal that helps your team win.

Unfortunately, my 500th goal, scored for the San Jose Sharks on November 10, 2007, was a brutal one. I shot the puck off the Plexiglas behind the net, and it caromed out front, hitting the goal post before Phoenix Coyotes goalie Alex Auld knocked it into his own net.

That's not the way you dream it will unfold, but I wasn't any less proud to score it. I was only the third American to reach 500 goals. Joe Mullen and Mike Modano were the others.

If you watch the video, you can see I was close to tears on the bench. If San Jose Sharks general manager Doug Wilson hadn't given me another chance when I was 37, I might have finished my career with 495 goals.

11. Becoming a 50-goal scorer

When I scored my 50th goal of the 1991–92 season, I felt as if it proved that I had become a superstar in the game. To score 50 in that era meant that you were among the best of the best, no questions asked. At 22, I was one of four 50-goal scorers that season. I was tied for seventh in the NHL scoring race, and led the NHL with 13 game-winning goals. I felt as if I was on top of the hockey world.

My 50-goal season was made more perfect by the fact that my 50th came in the Boston Garden in front of all of my family and friends from Massachusetts.

12. Meeting Mike Keenan in the bathroom in Montreal

It was the night before the NHL draft, and we were at a restaurant in old Montreal.

I went to the bathroom and there was Keenan standing at the urinal. According to the rumor mill, Keenan's Blackhawks were among those teams considering drafting me.

Stepping up to the urinal, I said hello to him. He knew who I was. "I hope you draft me," I said.

He asked me if I would play hard for him. He asked me if I had "big balls." I said that I did, joking that I could whip them out if he wanted me to prove it. That's a true story. Knowing him the way I do now, I'm sure he was impressed that I had the confidence to talk to him, even joke with him, in that way. I've always believed that impromptu meeting helped solidify in Keenan's mind that I was the guy to draft.

13. Punked in Hull, Quebec

Throughout my career, I was a player known as a practical joker. But I was the victim of one of the best practical jokes I ever saw in the hockey world.

It occurred in 1988, while I was playing for the Hull Olympiques. On a road trip to Chicoutimi, my teammates convinced me that the team had forgotten to secure the work pass I needed to enter the state park where the arena was located.

I was told I would have to sneak into the park by hiding in the baggage compartment of the bus. A few miles from the park, the bus stopped, and I climbed into the storage area with the smelly equipment bags.

After driving a few uncomfortable miles, the bus stopped and a voice outside ordered me out of the baggage compartment. I assumed it was the park marshal who had caught us. When the door opened, I must have looked like E.T. tucked into the closet with all the stuffed animals. But instead of the park marshal it was my coach Alain Vigneault and my teammates who were all laughing uncontrollably because I had been taken in by their initiation prank.

It was a great bonding exercise. And we all know that Vigneault has gone on to have great success as an NHL coach.

14. Proudly watching the Americans beat Canada in 1996

Although I could not play for Team USA at the 1996 World Cup of hockey because I was a free agent without a contract, I loved watching my boys take down Canada to win the championship. That has to be one of the proudest moments of my career. My feeling was that we officially became a hockey superpower in that tournament.

Before that tournament, I had told everyone that we were going to win the tournament. Team USA general manager Lou Lamoriello wasn't thrilled with me. But I believed our confidence level needed to be stated on the record. I never regretted making that prediction.

15. Being introduced to skating by a good neighbor

When I was born, my parents were not hockey fans. Far from it. But when we were living in Seymour, Connecticut, we had a neighbor who wanted to take her three-year-old son to skating lessons. She believed her son would quit if he didn't have a friend accompanying him and convinced my parents to let me take lessons as well. As it turned out, he liked it but I loved it. You couldn't get me out of the rink. I can't remember the neighbor's name, but I appreciate the contribution she made to my career. I may have never ended up in hockey if she hadn't persuaded my mother that I needed skating lessons.

16. Getting a taste of Mike Keenan's methods

I am probably the only athlete in world history to say that his coach's attempt to strangle him was one of the highlights of his career.

The story was featured prominently in my first book because it played such an important role in making me the player I became in the NHL. After bypassing several opportunities to throw a check in a preseason game in Kalamazoo, Michigan, Blackhawks coach Mike Keenan grabbed me around the throat and said in an expletive-laced tirade that I would never play a game in the NHL if I surrendered any more opportunities to throw a check.

His screaming was so intense that he was spitting all over my face. It was clear that I wasn't in high school anymore. I was deathly afraid that Keenan would sabotage my career.

On my next shift, I fired around the ice like a human cannon ball. That became my playing style. It was a moment that changed my life.

17. Almost making the 1988 U.S. Olympic team

After playing well in the USA Select 17 summer camp, U.S. Olympic coach Dave Peterson invited me to the 1988 Olympic training camp.

Peter Laviolette, now the Nashville Predators' coach, was my roommate. He helped me adjust to playing at a higher level. In my mind, I felt I played well enough to make the team.

Peterson agreed with that assessment—at least, that's what he implied when he cut me. He said he was only cutting me because I was too young. Peterson was concerned that leaving high school would not be good for me in the long term.

His decision pissed me off. It made me want to work harder to prove he had made a mistake. In hindsight, it probably was better for me that I returned to school. The U.S. team didn't have a good

1988 Olympic experience, and I managed to graduate high school early and turn professional with the Blackhawks.

18. Scoring a big goal against Ed Belfour

In 2003–04, I scored the Game 6 overtime goal for the Philadelphia Flyers that eliminated the Toronto Maple Leafs.

Because of concussions and injuries, it had been a tough season for me. But the goal against my former Chicago Blackhawks teammate was definitely one of the highlights of my career. It was my 51st career playoff goal. I played well in that postseason, finishing third on the Flyers in scoring with 13 points in 18 games.

When I scored that goal in Toronto, I felt as if we had a good shot to reach the Stanley Cup Final. That Flyers team was a talented group, led by Keith Primeau, Alex Zhamnov, Simon Gagne, John LeClair, Mark Recchi, Sami Kapanen, Michal Handzus, Kim Johnsson, and Danny Markov. Those Flyers may have been the most talented team I ever played with.

That's why it was such a major disappointment when we lost to the Tampa Bay Lightning in the next round. It felt like such a lost opportunity, especially after the Lightning won the Stanley Cup.

19. Being recruited by the Great One

In 1984–85, Wayne Gretzky recruited me to play for the Hull Olympiques team he owned in the Quebec Major Junior Hockey League. While his Edmonton Oilers were in Boston, Gretzky invited my family out to breakfast. We were his guests for a game at the Boston Garden.

Although I opted to stay at Thayer, I reached two important conclusions as a result of my meeting with the Great One.

First, I must have been a quality player, because Gretzky would not have recruited me if I wasn't. Second, seeing Gretzky without his shirt on in the dressing room convinced me I could play in the NHL. That was important for a 14-year-old NHL aspirant who only weighed 130 pounds at the time.

20. Watching the Blackhawks win the Stanley Cup in 2010

I will never apologize for being emotional on NBC when the Blackhawks won in 2010. Having played eight seasons in Chicago, I had always been disappointed that we couldn't deliver the Stanley Cup the fans desperately wanted. We had given all that we had but it wasn't enough. To see Chicago finally celebrating a Stanley Cup was gratifying. I received plenty of hate messages for being openly happy for the Blackhawks, particularly from Philadelphia fans who were deprived of the Stanley Cup that season.

But here's the absolute truth: I would have also cried if the Flyers had won. The Philadelphia fans treated me with great respect when I played there.

21. Playing in the Quebec Peewee Tournament

When you are a young player, going to the Quebec Peewee Tournament is like traveling to the holy land. You are told that Wayne Gretzky, Mario Lemieux, Marcel Dionne, and Guy Lafleur all played there when they were your age.

Teams come from all over the world to play there because it features the best 12- and 13-year-old players on the planet.

When you are a young American, the tournament seems cool and exotic because French is the primary language in the city. Hall of Fame defenseman Brad Park played in the first Quebec Peewee Tournament in 1960.

It remains one of my career highlights because in my second year at the tournament, I scored seven goals in a game for my Maryland team, the Junior Capitals. I think Gretzky scored nine goals in one game at this tournament. But when I scored seven, I started drawing notice as an elite player. People remember what you accomplish in the Quebec Peewee Tournament.

22. Receiving a second chance

In August of 2007, I thought my NHL career was kaput until San Jose Sharks general manager Doug Wilson called to say he wanted to talk about extending my career.

Wilson had been my first roommate in Chicago. He offered me the NHL minimum, but the money didn't matter because I would have played for nothing. I was just thrilled that an NHL team still wanted me.

He placed heavy stipulations on his offer: for example, I couldn't drink alcohol and I couldn't be the media's darling. No interviews whatsoever. He wanted my focus to be completely on hockey.

We were on the golf course when he spelled out the terms and conditions of the deal. To prove my sincerity, I poured out the beer I was holding. It had been a bad summer until Wilson called. I felt as if I was being washed out of a sport I loved because no one believed I could still play. Instead of me choosing to go out on my own terms,

NHL teams were making my decision for me. Wilson was giving me a chance to change that.

Following all of Wilson's rules, I scored 14 goals and played an important role on the team. In the playoffs, I had two goals and two assists in a Game 7 win against the Calgary Flames, coached by my old friend Mike Keenan. Given how despondent I was about how my career was ending, that first season in San Jose felt like a 50-goal season. Sometimes friends save you. That's what Wilson did for me.

23. Playing with Tony Amonte at Thayer Academy

Without a doubt, playing three seasons with Amonte in prep school helped my development as a hockey player. In my freshman season, Thayer upset Avon Old Farms, led by defenseman Brian Leetch, 6–4 to win the New England prep school tournament. Tony and I each scored a pair of goals in that game, and Leetch had two for Avon Old Farms.

In Massachusetts, people say there were more college and professional scouts at that game than any other game in high school hockey history. It would rank among my all-time favorite games. Arthur Valicenti was Thayer's coach, and he was a no-nonsense guy who taught me to be a complete player. I swear that he looked like he was an Italian mafia boss out of the movies.

Anyone who watched that game might have at least guessed it was possible that all three of us would end up in the U.S. Hockey Hall of Fame. That's how hard we competed in that game. I've always said that Amonte never received the attention he deserved for being the star he truly was. He scored 30 or more goals eight times in the NHL.

Here is a good story about Amonte when he played for USA at the 1996 World Championships: before the deciding game, U.S. coach Ron Wilson had stopped at Amonte's locker to tell him that he had a feeling that Amonte was going to emerge as the hero in the big game.

"Tony," Wilson said, "you are going to be America's Paul Henderson."

"Who the hell is Paul Henderson?" Amonte joked.

Everyone in hockey and Canada knows that Henderson had become a Canadian hero by scoring the deciding goal to give Canada a series triumph against the Soviet Union in the 1972 Summit Series.

But Amonte didn't want to be compared to a Canadian hero.

"Can I just be Mike Eruzione?" Amonte asked.

"Yeah," Wilson said. "You are both ugly, you are both Italian, and you are both from Boston University. You can be Eruzione and score the big goal for us tonight."

With 2:35 left in the third period, that conversation turned prophetic when Amonte tucked a shot under the crossbar to score the game-winning goal in a 5–2 victory.

24. Playing with Modano and Amonte at the World Junior Championships

As a teenager, I played on a line with Tony Amonte and Mike Modano at the World Junior Championships. I'm guessing that's the most accomplished American line in WJC history.

We could all thunder up the ice like we were NASCARs on the backstretch at Daytona.

I can't say it was the most dynamic line in WJC history, because when we played against Russia we matched up against Alexander Mogilny, Pavel Bure, and Sergei Fedorov. Holy shit they were talented. Every shift we were on the ice, it was like we were traveling at the speed of light. This was NHL speed in a junior game.

In my two WJC appearances, I set an American record with 25 points. It was eventually broken, but three appearances at the WJC were needed to better the numbers I produced in two appearances.

25. Retiring with dignity

Thanks to the San Jose Sharks, I was able to end my career on a high note. They gave me an opportunity to play two extra seasons in a fun environment. They handled my retirement announcement with overflowing class and professionalism. Because of the way everything was handled, I've never had any regrets about my retirement. I feel as if I retired at the right time and with the right amount of attention. I had always wanted to leave the game with style, and the Sharks helped me accomplish that objective.

I shed tears during my retirement press conference, but how could I not? My friends Keith Tkachuk, Mike Modano, and Chris Chelios all called in to pay tribute.

Then Wilson said this: "[Roenick] is one of the greatest hockey players to play this game. He played hard. He was fearless. He'd go through the wall. I've had guys come up to me and say he was the greatest teammate they ever had."

That may have been the best compliment I ever received, and it came on my last day as an NHL player. That's exactly how I wanted to leave the game.

26. Being coached by my dad

Hey, it wasn't always easy having my dad be overly invested in my career. But I also recognize that I wouldn't be where I am today if not for having parents who pushed me to be the best I could be. It's a fine line between motivating and infuriating. My father made plenty of sacrifices and spent thousands upon thousands of dollars to give me the best opportunity to become an elite player. He gave up his fun life so that I could have a fun life. He taught me to be a winner. He taught me how to deal with losing. I will never be able to repay him for the contributions he made.

27. Being hired as an analyst by NBC

When NBC executive producer Sam Flood hired me to be an analyst, he must have felt like a wrangler trying to break a wild stallion. He knew he was signing a maverick. I'm not afraid to shoot my mouth off. In television, that can be both a blessing and a curse.

I'm overwhelmingly thankful that NBC has given me the opportunity to stay involved in a game that I love.

I feel blessed that I've maintained relevancy in this sport. It's like I used to have one of the best jobs on the planet, and then I retired and found another job that is equally fun and rewarding. I can do this job until I'm old and feeble, as long as all of those concussions I've had don't come back to bite me. Just writing about it reminds me how fortunate I've been in my career. How lucky can one man be?

FOURTEEN

A YEAR
IN THE LIFE

CHAPTER FOURTEEN

A Year in the Life

When I retired from the NHL in 2009, I realized quickly that I don't know how to stop dreaming big.

Most top NHL goal-scorers would agree that one of the keys to finding the net on a regular basis is to crave greatness. You need an intense desire to want to accomplish something memorable every time you are on the ice.

You don't score more than 500 goals in your career by meeting minimum requirements. You become a premium goal-scorer by pushing yourself to explore the outer limits of your ability.

When some players saw a small opening in the defense, I would see a major scoring opportunity. If you want to be a top performer, you must expand your vision beyond what's happening in front of you. You have to widen your horizon. You have to anticipate what will happen next and understand how you can change the course of events. You have to be driven to seize the moment, to make it your time to be a difference-maker.

That's the way my brain processed information when I was a professional athlete, and that line of thinking has followed me into civilian life.

Since I played my last season with the San Jose Sharks, I can't shake the feeling that I should be chasing a monumental achievement outside of the hockey world or even television.

For years now, I've thought about ways I can use my personality and talent to help people. At some point, I want to take a year out of my life and spend it raising money for people who really need it.

My plan would be to travel around the country in an RV, visiting 52 cities in 52 weeks. I would spend one year on the road with the sole purpose of raising money that can be distributed to the truly needy.

It's difficult to predict how much I could raise. Even if I only raised $200,000 per city, I would end up with more than $10 million. Obviously, I believe I can raise much more than that. A conservative guess is that I could raise between $10 and $20 million. But I wouldn't be shocked if I exceeded $20 million.

My hope is that I could find philanthropists who would match what I raised.

Charity has always appealed to me, but I've always felt that my contributions have been too impersonal. Yes, I can participate in or even host a one-day charity golf tournament and raise money and send a check to the American Cancer Society or the Make-a-Wish Foundation. But what happens after the check leaves your hand? Where does the money go? Is the money going directly to people who need it?

The one-day events are valuable, because many of those fine charitable causes couldn't survive without them. But I want to do more. I need to talk to the people who need help. I want them to tell me what it's like to walk in their shoes. I want to figure out if there is more that I can do to help. I need to understand why society has the problems it does.

I made a great living during my hockey career playing a game I love. I'm thankful for what I have, and I feel as if I need to give something back. I need to make a major effort to make life better for others.

As a former athlete and a television personality, I have the ability to raise large amounts of money. I travel in circles where people are not living paycheck to paycheck. I have relationships with rich, well-connected people. I'm involved in charitable causes now, but I feel as if I should do more than I am.

It's not about hosting another golf tournament or having my own charity. I'm looking to do something that creates real change in the lives of others.

The Jeremy Roenick RV Tour might be able to accomplish that.

The idea would be to plan one major fund-raising event in each city. For example, when I go to Detroit, I would ask my buddy Kid Rock to play a concert to raise money. When I'm in Seattle, I will ask my buddy Eddie Vedder from Pearl Jam to do the same. And you can bet that I will be asking my buddies such as Charles Barkley, Michael Jordan, and Wayne Gretzky to help me out in whatever city they are in.

But I want to do as much as I can face to face. I'm willing to go door to door and ask for donations. I'm going to stand on street corners. I'm going to visit the movers and shakers in every town. I'm going to ask people to give whatever they can afford, whether it's pocket change or a six-figure check.

I'm going to stand in the middle of a mall parking lot with a megaphone and ask people to throw whatever they can spare into a large barrel. I'm going to shake hands, sign autographs, pose for photos, and do whatever people want me to do in order to get a donation.

If the Chicago-area McDonald's restaurants agree to give a percentage of their daily take to my charity effort, I will work their drive-thrus all day. If Tim Hortons wants to give a charitable donation, I will show up a 4:00 AM to make doughnuts.

I will jump into Lake Michigan in the dead of winter for a large donation.

Tracy always tells me that I have a large collection of friends, and I've never asked anyone to do anything for me. But that will change if I embark on this quest. I will call everyone I know and ask them for help and/or money.

I am going to call NHL commissioner Gary Bettman and ask him to write me a check. Don't think I won't. To be honest, Bettman would probably be the first guy who would write me a check, because that's who he is.

My former coach Mike Keenan will get a call as well. If he gives me $100 for every time he yelled at me in my first 100 games with the Blackhawks, I will be off to a good start.

The band Nickelback is from Vancouver, and the guys in that band love their hockey. I'm sure if I called lead vocalist Chad Kroeger, he would do something for me.

The great crooner Michael Buble is a hockey fan, and you can bet he will get a call.

Unquestionably there will be a hockey component to this tour. I'm sure that my RV will roll into a parking lot at every NHL arena for a game. Hopefully, NHL team officials will allow me to bring my big barrel onto their concourses. I will sign autographs as long as people keep filling up the barrel.

Anyone who makes a donation will receive, in addition to my eternal gratitude, my pledge that all of their money is going to someone who truly needs the cash.

While I'm collecting money, I'm also going to be looking for people whose lives could be improved by a helping financial hand. I'll be looking for people who are trying to raise money to pay for transplants. I'll be looking to help the single mom who is working two jobs but still can't afford to send her children to college. I'll be looking to help veterans whose lives have been affected by combat. I'll be trying to find the doctor who operates a free clinic in a poverty-stricken area. I'll be giving help to battered women to help them start a new life. I hope to give some grants to homeless shelters and soup kitchens.

What I'm really hoping is that people will tell me about needy people who are too proud to seek help.

I also will be looking to help teenagers who have suffered debilitating injuries while playing sports. My association with Jack Jablonski is one of my primary motivations for the tour. My initial objective was to raise money to help Jack after he was paralyzed. But I might be getting more out of our relationship now than he is getting. Knowing him has enhanced my life immensely.

I believe this tour could be life-altering for me, as well as for the people we help. How many other inspirational people like Jack

Jablonski are out there? If I can figure out how to make this tour work, I bet I will find many others like Jack. I will locate people who will make vital contributions to life if we can just give them some temporary help.

I would also hope to persuade a television network to be involved in some capacity. I plan to investigate whether one of them would be interested in filming the tour for a reality series. More exposure will help us raise more money. Plus, imagine the entertainment value of following yours truly around in an RV for a year.

Obviously, I have not worked out all of the details, but it would likely start on January 1 at the Winter Classic. If I was looking to make the biggest splash, I would end it on New Year's Eve in New York's Times Square. But that isn't what I'm planning. I would love to spend the last day of the tour on the beach near my home in San Diego, California, surrounded by my family and close friends.

One thing I am sure of is that an accounting firm like Ernst and Young would be hired to insure that all the money collected was properly recorded and distributed. You cannot begin an undertaking of this magnitude without having professional oversight to make sure that rules are followed and money is safeguarded. I will be there in person when money is collected, but I won't be involved in the handling of it. In fact, I don't want to be told how much we have collected until the tour is completed. No one except the folks from the accounting firm will know the final total until the tour is over.

It's likely that I will also put together an advisory board to help me decide who should receive the money. Some decisions will be obvious, but it may be challenging to decide where the final grants should go. I'm not naïve. I know I cannot help everyone.

I'm hoping my effort will inspire others to pick up the torch and do what they can to help. While I'm interesting in providing immediate help to people, I'm also hoping that we can come up with some ideas for long-term solutions to the problems we face today.

The sticking point in this entire plan is timing. I would need at least a year to plan this event, and I have to pick the right time to drop out of my career. I need to do this fairly soon because I want to take advantage of my relevancy. Many fans still remember me as a player, and I'm on television enough to remain recognizable and newsworthy.

Plus, at 45, I'm still young and vibrant enough to be an entertaining force on a year-long tour.

The argument against embarking on this crusade is that I'm in the midst of a strong career at NBC. Plus, I have hopes of returning to an NHL team as a member of its front office.

How do I factor all of that in? That's the issue that I'm currently debating in my mind. What's my window for this? I don't have an answer.

What I am sure of is this: I'm the man who can pull off an event of this magnitude. I've always viewed myself as someone who can do things that ordinary people wouldn't do. I'm not hindered by self-doubt. I always expect to succeed in everything I do. I'm not afraid of failure. I'm fueled by my desire not to fail. I came back quicker from injury than most players. I played through high levels of pain. I played through broken bones. I am a highly motivated human being.

Plus, I handle rattlesnakes without fear.

That's right. I pick up rattlesnakes. Folks at the famed Cascata Golf Course in Boulder City, Nevada, still tell the story of my encounter with a rattlesnake on that course several years ago.

Playing with several members of the San Jose Sharks, I spotted a rattlesnake wriggling across the cart path. My caddie was horrified when I climbed out of the cart and headed toward the venomous creature.

"Leave it alone!" he screamed.

When I picked up the rattler, the caddie backpedaled 10 steps. Wanting to show the snake to my teammates who were playing ahead of me, I tossed it in our cooler.

After I completed my last three holes, I carried the cooler to where the boys were drinking and opened it up. When the rattlesnake slithered out, the guys ran in five or six different directions. Records were set in the 40-yard dash.

Keep in mind that I have lived in Arizona for a long time and I have seen many, many rattlesnakes. I know what I'm doing. I brought one into my house once and Tracy almost went up a wall.

Today when I golf with my buddies in Arizona, they say they will only agree to play 18 holes with me if I agree not to play with the rattlesnakes.

Maybe that's why I have the confidence to pull off what could be the biggest one-man charity drive the world has ever seen.

Who is going to say no to someone who can score 513 NHL goals *and* handle a rattlesnake?